THE CHRISTIAN'S SECRET

OF A

HAPPY LIFE

COMPLETE AND UNABRIDGED

HANNAH
WHITALL SMITH

BARBOUR
PUBLISHING

THE
CHRISTIAN'S
SECRET
OF A
HAPPY LIFE

© 1998 by Barbour Publishing, Inc.

ISBN 1-59310-707-2

The text of this book is in the public domain and may be used freely. This typesetting, however, is the property of Barbour Publishing, Inc., and may not be reproduced for any usage, commercial or noncommercial.

All scripture quotations are taken from the King James Version of the Bible.

Published by Barbour Publishing, Inc., P.O. Box 719, Uhrichsville, Ohio 44683
www.barbourbooks.com

Our mission is to publish and distribute inspirational products offering exceptional value and biblical encouragement to the masses.

ecpa Member of the
Evangelical Christian
Publishers Association

Printed in the United States of America.

Contents

HANNAH WHITALL SMITH (1832–1911)

Hannah Whitall Smith is best remembered as the author of one of the most popular devotional books of all time, *The Christian's Secret of a Happy Life.*

Born into a strict Quaker home in Pennsylvania in 1832, Hannah Whitall suffered from deep spiritual doubts during her early years. Her inner struggle continued into her marriage to Robert Piersall Smith in 1851, but in 1858 the couple committed their lives to Christ and decided to leave the Quaker faith to join the Plymouth Brethren.

A further spiritual experience in 1867 led Hannah and Robert to undertake a speaking tour on the "Higher Christian Life" in the United States and Europe. As Robert's health declined, the couple stayed in England and observed the 1874 founding of the Keswick Convention. It was at a Keswick conference in 1886 that Amy Carmichael would feel the call of God to the mission field.

Hannah Whitall Smith penned *The Christian's Secret of a Happy Life* in 1875 and wrote eighteen other books, as well, including *The Unselfishness of God and How I Discovered It* in 1903. She was active in the Women's Christian Temperance Union, supported women's suffrage and other issues of sexual equality, and studied the various religious movements that blossomed in the late nineteenth century.

Smith was stricken with arthritis for the last seven years of her life and was ultimately confined to a wheelchair, but she still entertained admirers of her writings. She died in 1911.

PREFACE

What I have to tell in this little book is no new story. The early church taught it in the days of the apostles, and from those days, down to the present time, there have been found in every age some whose voices and whose lives have proclaimed it.

Many times it has been lost sight of, and the church has seemed to fall into almost hopeless darkness and lifelessness. But the "secret" has always been preserved by an apostolic succession of those who have walked and talked with God.

In the present day the truth concerning it has been afresh revived, and this book is an effort to tell it again in a way that will be simple enough for all to understand. Too often the language of religion, like the oft repeated chimes of a bell, seems to lose its power to attract attention; and it may be that even a bell of inferior tone shall be able to break the careless inattention of some souls.

I have not tried, therefore, to make my book theological. I could not if I would. I have simply sought to tell the blessed story, so old and yet so new, in the homely and familiar words of everyday life.

I do not want to change the theological views of a single individual. The truths I have to tell are not theological, but practical. They are, I believe, the fundamental truths of life and experience, the truths that underlie all theologies and that are in fact their real and vital meaning. They will fit in with every creed, simply making it possible for those who hold the creed to live up to their own beliefs and to find in them the experimental realities of a present Savior and a present salvation.

Most of us acknowledge that there is behind all religions

an absolute religion that holds the vital truth of each, and it is of this absolute religion my book seeks to treat.

No doubt it is very imperfectly done, but I can only trust that all its mistakes may be counteracted, and only that which is true may find entrance into any heart. The book is sent out in tender sympathy and yearning love for all struggling, weary souls, of whatever creed or name; and its message goes right from my heart to theirs. I have given the best I have and can do no more.

This new and revised issue goes forth on its mission with the prayer that the Lord may continue to use it as a voice to teach some, who sorely need it, the true "secret of a happy life."

H.W.S.

PHILADELPHIA, *January 1888*

THE CRY OF SAINT PAUL
Brethren, my heart's desire and prayer to God for Israel is, that they might be saved.
ROMANS 10:1

Oh, could I tell, ye surely would believe it!
    Oh, could I only say what I have seen!
How should I tell, or how can ye receive it,
    How, till He bringeth you where I have been?
Therefore, O Lord, I will not fail nor falter;
    Nay but I ask it, nay but I desire,
Lay on my lips thine embers of the altar,
    Seal with the ring, and furnish with the fire.
Give me a voice, a cry, and a complaining—
    Oh, let my sound be stormy in their ears!

Throat that would shout, but cannot stay for
    straining;
Eyes that would weep, but cannot wait for
    tears.
Quick, in a moment, infinite forever,
    Send an arousal better than I pray;
Give me a grace upon the faint endeavor,
    Souls for my hire, and Pentecost today!
Scarcely I catch the words of His revealing,
    Hardly I hear Him, dimly understand;
Only the Power that is within me pealing,
    Lives on my lips, and beckons with my hand.
Whoso has felt the Spirit of the Highest,
    Cannot confound, nor doubt Him, nor deny;
Yea, with one voice, O world, though thou deniest,
    Stand thou on the side, for on this am I.

F.W.H. Myers

PART I
THE LIFE

Chapter 1

Is It Scriptural?

No thoughtful person can question the fact that, for the most part, the Christian life, as it is generally lived, is not entirely a happy life. A keen observer once said to me, "You Christians seem to have a religion that makes you miserable. You are like a man with a headache. He does not want to get rid of his head, but it hurts him to keep it. You cannot expect outsiders to seek very earnestly for anything so uncomfortable." Then for the first time I saw, as in a flash, that the religion of Christ ought to be and was meant to be, to its possessors, not something to make them miserable but something to make them happy; and I began then and there to ask the Lord to show me the secret of a happy Christian life.

It is this secret, so far as I have learned it, that I shall try to tell in the following pages.

All of God's children, I am convinced, feel instinctively, in their moments of divine illumination, that a life of inward rest and outward victory is their unalienable birthright. Can you remember, some of you, the shout of triumph your souls gave when you first became acquainted with the Lord Jesus and had a glimpse of His mighty saving power? How sure you were of victory then! How easy it seemed to be more than conquerors through Him that loved you! Under the leadership of a captain who had never been foiled in battle, how could you dream of defeat!

And yet, to many of you, how different has been your real experience! Your victories have been few and fleeting, your defeats many and disastrous. You have not lived as you feel children of God ought to live. You have had perhaps a clear understanding of doctrinal truths, but you have not come into possession of their life and power. You have rejoiced in your knowledge of the things revealed in the scriptures but have not had a living realization of the things themselves, consciously felt in the soul. Christ is believed in, talked about, and served, but He is not known as the soul's actual and very life, abiding there forever and revealing Himself there continually in His beauty. You have found Jesus as your Savior from the penalty of sin, but you have not found Him as your Savior from its power. You have carefully studied the Holy scriptures and have gathered much precious truth therefrom, which you have trusted would feed and nourish your spiritual life, but in spite of it all, your souls are starving and dying within you, and you cry out in secret, again and again, for that bread and water of life which you see promised in the scriptures to all believers.

In the very depths of your hearts, you know that your experience is not a scriptural experience; that, as an old writer said, your religion is "but a *talk* to what the early Christians enjoyed, possessed, and lived in." And your hearts have sunk within you, as, day after day, and year after year, your early visions of triumph have seemed to grow more and more dim, and you have been forced to settle down to the conviction, that the best you can expect from your religion is a life of alternate failure and victory, one hour sinning, and the next repenting, and then beginning again, only to fail again, and again to repent.

But *is* this all? Had the Lord Jesus only this in His mind when He laid down His precious life to deliver you from your sore and cruel bondage to sin? Did He propose to Himself only this partial deliverance? Did He intend to leave you thus struggling under a weary consciousness of defeat and discouragement? Did He fear that a continuous victory would dishonor Him and bring reproach on His name? When all those declarations were made concerning His coming and the work He was to accomplish, did they mean only this that you have experienced? Was there a hidden reserve in each promise, that was meant to deprive it of its complete fulfillment? Did "delivering us out of the hand of our enemies" mean that they should still have dominion over us? Did "enabling us always to triumph" mean that we were only to triumph sometimes? Did being made "more than conquerors through him that loved us" mean constant defeat and failure? Does being "saved to the uttermost" mean the meager salvation we see manifested among us now? Can we dream that the Savior, who was wounded for our transgressions and bruised for our iniquities, could possibly see of the travail of His soul and be satisfied in such Christian lives as fill the Church today? The Bible tells us that "for this purpose the Son of God was manifested, that he might destroy the works of the devil"; and can we imagine for a moment that this is beyond His power and that He finds Himself unable to accomplish the thing He was manifested to do?

In the very outset, then, settle down on this one thing, that Jesus came to save you, now, in this life, from the power and dominion of sin and to make you more than conquerors through His power. If you doubt this, search your Bible, and collect together every announcement or declaration concerning the purposes and object of his death on the cross. You will be astonished to find how full they are. Everywhere and always, His work is said to be to deliver us from our sins, from our bondage, from our defilement; and not a hint is given, anywhere, that this deliverance was to be only the limited and partial one with which Christians so continually try to be satisfied.

Let me give you the teaching of scripture on this subject. When the angel of the Lord appeared unto Joseph in a dream and announced the coming birth of the Savior, he said, "And thou shalt call his name JESUS: for he shall save his people from their sins."

When Zacharias was "filled with the Holy Ghost" at the birth of his son, and "prophesied," he declared that God had visited his people in order to fulfill the promise and the oath He had made them; which promise was, "that he would grant unto us, that we being delivered out of the hand of our enemies might serve him without fear, in holiness and righteousness before him, all the days of our life."

When Peter was preaching in the porch of the temple to the wondering Jews, he said, "Unto you first God, having raised up his Son Jesus, sent him to bless you, in turning away every one of you from his iniquities."

When Paul was telling to the Ephesian church the wondrous truth, that Christ had so loved them as to give Himself for them, he went on to declare that His purpose in thus doing was, "that he might sanctify and cleanse it with the washing of water by the word, that he might present it to himself a glorious church, not having spot, or wrinkle, or any such thing; but that it should be holy and without blemish."

When Paul was seeking to instruct Titus, his own son after the common faith, concerning the grace of God, he declared that the object of that grace was to teach us "that, denying ungodliness and worldly lusts, we should live soberly, righteously, and godly, in this present world"; and adds, as the reason of this, that Christ "gave himself for us, that he might redeem us from all iniquity, and purify unto himself a peculiar people, zealous of good works."

When Peter was urging upon the Christians, to whom he was writing, a holy and Christlike walk, he tells them that "even hereunto were ye called: because Christ also suffered for us, leaving us an example, that ye should follow his steps: who did no sin, neither was guile found in his mouth"; and adds, "Who his own self bare our sins in his own body on the tree, that we, being dead to sins, should live unto righteousness: by whose stripes ye were healed."

When Paul was contrasting in the Ephesians the walk suitable for a Christian with the walk of an unbeliever, he sets before them the truth in Jesus as being this. "That ye put off concerning the former conversation the old man, which is corrupt according to the deceitful lusts; and be renewed in the spirit of your mind; and that ye put on the new man, which after God is created in righteousness and true holiness."

And when, in Romans 6, he was answering forever the question as to a child of God continuing in sin and showing how utterly foreign it was to the whole spirit and aim of the salvation of Jesus, he brings up the fact of our judicial death and resurrection with Christ, as an unanswerable argument for our practical deliverance from it and says, "God forbid. How shall we, that are dead to sin, live any longer therein? Know ye not, that so many of us as were baptized into Jesus Christ were baptized into his death? Therefore we are buried with him by baptism into death: that like as Christ was raised up from the dead by the glory of the Father, even so we also should walk in newness of life," and adds, "Knowing this, that our old man is crucified with him, that the body of sin might be destroyed, that henceforth we should not serve sin."

It is a fact sometimes overlooked that, in the declarations concerning the object of the death of Christ, far more mention is made of a present salvation from sin than of a future salvation in a heaven beyond, showing plainly God's estimate of the relative importance of these two things.

Dear Christians, will you receive the testimony of the scripture on this matter? The same crucial questions that troubled the Church in Paul's day are troubling it now: first, "Shall we continue in sin, that grace may abound?" and second, "Do we then make void the law through faith?" Shall our answer to these be Paul's emphatic "God forbid," and his triumphant assertions that, instead of making it void, "we establish the law"; and that "what the law could not do, in that it was weak through the flesh, God sending his own Son in the likeness of sinful flesh, and for sin, condemned sin in the flesh: that the righteousness of the law might be fulfilled in us, who walk not after the flesh, but after the Spirit."

Can we, for a moment, suppose that the holy God, who hates sin in the sinner, is willing to tolerate it in the Christian, and that He has even arranged the plan of salvation in such a way as to make it impossible for those who are saved from the guilt of sin to find deliverance from its power?

As Dr. Chalmers well says, "Sin is that scandal which must be rooted out from the great spiritual household over which the Divinity rejoices. . . . Strange administration, indeed, for sin to be so hateful to God as to lay all who had incurred it under death, and yet, when readmitted into life, that sin should be permitted; and that what was before the object of destroying vengeance should now become the object of an upheld and protected toleration. Now that the penalty is taken off, think you it is possible that the unchangeable God has so given up His antipathy to sin as that man, ruined and redeemed man, may now perseveringly indulge, under the new arrangement, in that which under the old destroyed him? Does not the God who loved righteousness and hated iniquity six thousand years ago, bear the same love to righteousness and hatred to iniquity still? . . . I now breathe the air of loving-kindness from heaven and can walk before God in peace and graciousness; shall I again attempt the incompatible alliance of two principles so adverse as that of an approving God and a persevering sinner? How shall we, recovered from so awful a catastrophe, continue that which first involved us in it? The cross of Christ, by the same mighty and decisive stroke wherewith it moved the curse of sin away from us, also surely moves away the power and the love of it from over us."

And not Dr. Chalmers only, but many other holy men of his generation and of our own, as well as of generations long past, have united in declaring that the redemption accomplished for us by our Lord Jesus Christ on the cross at Calvary is a redemption from the power of sin as well as from its guilt, and that He *is* able to save to the uttermost all who come unto God by Him.

A quaint old Quaker divine of the seventeenth century says: "There is nothing so contrary to God as sin, and God will not suffer sin always to rule His masterpiece, man. When we consider the infiniteness of God's power for destroying that which is contrary to Him, who can believe that the devil must always stand and prevail?

"I believe it is inconsistent and disagreeable with the true faith for people to be Christians and yet to believe that Christ, the eternal Son of God, to whom all power in heaven and earth is given, will suffer sin and the devil to have dominion over them.

"But you will say no man by all the power he hath can redeem himself, and no man can live without sin. We will say Amen to it. But if men tell us that when God's power comes to help us and to redeem us out of sin, it cannot be effected, then this doctrine we cannot away with; nor I hope you neither.

"Would you approve of it if I should tell you that God puts forth His power to do such a thing, but the devil hinders Him? That it is impossible for God to do it, because the devil does not like it? That it is impossible that any one should be free from sin, because the devil hath got such a power in them that God cannot cast him out? This is lamentable doctrine, yet hath not this been preached? It doth in plain terms say, though God doth interpose His power, it is impossible, because the devil hath so rooted sin in the nature of man. Is not man God's creature, and cannot He new make him and cast sin out of him? If you say sin is deeply rooted in man, I say so, too; yet not so deeply rooted but Christ Jesus hath entered so deeply into the root of the nature of man that He hath received power to destroy the devil and his works and to recover and redeem man into righteousness and holiness. Or else it is false that 'He is able to save to the uttermost all that come unto God by Him.' We must throw away the Bible if we say that it is impossible for God to deliver man out of sin.

"We know," he continues, "when our friends are in captivity, as in Turkey or elsewhere, we pay our money for their redemption; but we will not pay our money if they be kept in their fetters still. Would not any one think himself cheated to pay so much money for their redemption and the bargain be made so that he shall be *said* to be redeemed and be *called* a redeemed captive, but he must wear his fetters still? How long? As long as he hath a day to live. This is for bodies, but now I am speaking of souls. Christ must be made to me redemption and rescue me from captivity. Am I a prisoner anywhere? Yes, verily, verily, he that committeth sin, saith Christ, he is a servant of sin, he is a slave of sin. If thou hast sinned, thou art a slave, a captive that must be redeemed out of captivity. Who will pay a price for me? I am poor; I have nothing; I cannot redeem myself: who will pay a price for me? There is one come who hath paid a price for me. That is well; that is good news; then I hope I shall come out of my captivity. What is His name? Is He called a redeemer? So, then, I do expect the benefit of my redemption and that I shall go out of my captivity. No, say they, you must abide in sin as long as you live. What! Must we never be delivered? Must this crooked heart and perverse will always remain? Must I be a believer and yet have no faith that reacheth to sanctification and holy living? Is there no mastery to be had, no getting victory over sin? Must it prevail over me as long as I live? What sort of a redeemer, then, is this, or what benefit have I in this life, of my redemption?"

Similar extracts might be quoted from Marshall and Romaine and many others to show that this doctrine is no new one in the church, however much it may have been lost sight of by the present generation of believers. It is the same old story that has filled with songs of triumph the daily lives of many saints of God, both Catholic and Protestant, throughout all ages; and it is now being sounded forth afresh to the unspeakable joy of weary and burdened souls.

Do not reject it then, dear reader, until you have prayerfully searched the scriptures to see whether these things be indeed so. Ask God to open the eyes of your understanding by His Spirit that you may know "what is the exceeding greatness of his power to us-ward who believe, according to the working of his mighty power, which he wrought in Christ, when he raised him from the dead, and set him at his own right hand in the heavenly places." And when you have begun to have some faint glimpses of this power, learn to look away utterly from your own weakness, and, putting your case into His hands, trust Him to deliver you.

"When thou goest out to battle against thine enemies, and seest horses, and chariots, and a people more than thou, be not afraid of them: for the LORD thy God is with thee, which brought thee up out of the land of Egypt. And it shall be, when ye are come nigh unto the battle, that the priest shall approach and speak unto the people, and shall say unto them, Hear, O Israel, ye approach this day unto battle against your enemies: let not your hearts faint, fear not, and do not tremble, neither be ye terrified because of them; for the LORD your God is he that goeth with you, to fight for you against your enemies, to save you." Deut 20:3

Chapter 2

God's Side and Man's Side

Much misunderstanding arises, in reference to this subject of the life and walk of faith, from the fact that its two sides are not clearly seen. People are apt to think that there is only one side to it, and, dwelling exclusively upon the one they happen to see the most clearly, without even a thought of any other, it is no wonder that distorted views of the whole matter are the legitimate consequence.

Now, there are two very decided and distinct sides to this subject, and, like all other subjects, it cannot be fully understood unless both of these sides are kept constantly in view. I refer of course to God's side and man's side; or, in other words, to God's part in the work of sanctification and man's part. These are very distinct and even contrasting but, although to a cursory observer they may sometimes so appear, they are not really contradictory.

At one time this was strikingly illustrated to me. There were two teachers of this interior life holding meetings in the same place, at alternate hours. One spoke only of God's part in the work, and the other dwelt exclusively upon man's part. They were both in perfect sympathy with each other and realized fully that they were each teaching different sides

THE CHRISTIAN'S SECRET OF A HAPPY LIFE

of the same great truth; and this also was understood by a large proportion of their hearers. But with some of the hearers it was different, and one lady said to me in the greatest perplexity, "I cannot understand it all. Here are two preachers undertaking to teach just the same truth, and yet to me they seem flatly to contradict each other." And I felt at the time that she expressed a puzzle that, very often, causes great difficulty in the minds of many honest inquirers after this truth.

Suppose two friends go to see some celebrated building and return home to describe it. One has seen only the north side and the other only the south. The first says: "The building was built in such a manner, and has such and such stories and ornaments." "Oh no," says the other, interrupting him, "you are altogether mistaken; I saw the building, and it was built in quite a different manner, and its ornaments and stories were so and so." A lively dispute might follow upon the truth of the respective descriptions until the two friends should discover that they had been describing different *sides* of the building, and then all would be reconciled at once.

I would like to state, as clearly as I can, what I judge to be the two distinct sides in this matter; and to show how looking at one, without seeing the other, will be sure to create wrong impressions and views of the truth.

To state it in brief, I would say, that man's part is to trust, and God's part is to work; and it can be seen at a glance how these two parts contrast with each other and yet are not necessarily contradictory. I mean this: there is certain *work* to be accomplished. We are to be delivered from the power of sin and are to be made perfect in every good work to do the will of God. "Beholding as in a glass the glory of the Lord," we are to be actually "changed into the same image from glory to glory, even as by the Spirit of the Lord." We are to be transformed by the renewing of our minds, that we may prove what is that good and acceptable and perfect will of God.

A real work is to be wrought in us and upon us. Besetting sins are to be conquered; evil habits are to be overcome; wrong dispositions and feelings are to be rooted out; and holy tempers and emotions are to be begotten. A positive transformation is to take place. So at least the Bible teaches.

Now, somebody must do this. Either we must do it for ourselves, or another must do it for us. We have most of us tried to do it for ourselves at first, and have grievously failed; then we discover, from the scriptures and from our own experience, that it is something we are unable to do, but that the Lord Jesus Christ has come on purpose to do it, and that He will do it for all who put themselves wholly into His hands and trust Him without reserve.

Now, under these circumstances, what is the part of the believer, and what is the part of the Lord? Plainly the believer can do nothing but trust; while the Lord, in whom he trusts, actually does the work entrusted to Him. *Trusting* and *doing* are certainly contrasted things, often indeed contradictory; but are they contradictory in this case? Manifestly not, because it is two different parties that are concerned. If we should say of one party in a transaction, that he trusted his case to another and yet attended to it himself, we should state a contradiction and an impossibility, but, when we say of two parties in a transaction, that one trusts the other to do something, and that the other goes to work and does it, we are stating something that is perfectly simple and harmonious. When we say, therefore, that, in this higher life, man's part is to trust, and God's part is to do the thing entrusted to Him, we do not surely present any very difficult or puzzling problem.

The preacher, who is speaking on man's part in the matter,

cannot speak of anything but surrender and trust, because this is positively all the man can do. We all agree about this. And yet such preachers are constantly criticized as though, in saying this, they had meant to imply there *was* no other part, and that therefore nothing but trusting is to be done. And the cry goes out that this doctrine of faith does away with all realities, that souls are just told to trust, and there is the end of it, and that they sit down thenceforward in a sort of religious easy chair, dreaming away a life, fruitless of any actual result. All this misapprehension arises, of course, from the fact that either the preacher has neglected to state, or the hearer has failed to hear the other side of the matter, which is, that when we trust, the Lord works, and that a great deal is done, not by us, but by Him. Actual results are reached by our trusting, because our Lord undertakes the thing entrusted to Him and accomplishes it. *We* do not do anything, but *He* does it, and it is all the more effectually done because of this. As soon as this is clearly seen, the difficulty as to the preaching of faith disappears entirely.

On the other hand, the preacher who dwells on God's part in the matter is criticized on a totally different ground. He does not speak of trust, for the Lord's part is not to trust but to work. The Lord's part is to *do* the thing entrusted to Him. He disciplines and trains by inward exercises and outward providences. He brings to bear upon us all the refining and purifying resources of His wisdom and His love. He makes everything in our lives and circumstances subservient to the one great purpose of causing us to grow in grace and of conforming us, day by day and hour by hour to the image of Christ. He carries us through a process of transformation, longer or shorter as our peculiar case may require, making actual and experimental the results for which we have trusted.

We have dared, for instance, according to the command in Romans 6:11, by faith to reckon ourselves dead unto sin. The Lord makes this a reality and puts us to death by a thousand little mortifications and crosses to the natural man. Our reckoning is available only because God thus makes it real. And yet the preacher who dwells upon this practical side of the matter and tells of God's processes for making faith's reckonings experimental realities may be accused of contradicting the preaching of faith altogether and of declaring only a process of gradual sanctification by works and of setting before the soul an impossible and hopeless task.

Now, sanctification is both a step of faith and a process of works. It is a step of surrender and trust on our part, and it is a process of development on God's part. By a step of faith we get into Christ; by a process we are made to "grow up into Him in all things." By a step of faith we put ourselves into the hands of the Divine Potter; by a gradual process He makes us into a vessel unto His own honor, meet for His use and prepared to every good work.

To illustrate this, suppose I were to describe to a person, who was entirely ignorant of the subject, the way in which a lump of clay is made into a beautiful vessel. I tell him first the part of the clay in the matter; and all I can say about this is that the clay is put into the potter's hands and then lies passive there, submitting itself to all the turnings and overturnings of the potter's hands upon it. There is really nothing else to be said about the clay's part. But could my hearer argue from this that nothing else is done, because I say that this is all the clay can do? If he is an intelligent hearer, he will not dream of doing so but will say, "I understand; this is what the clay must do. But what must the potter do?"

"Ah," I answer, "now we come to the important part. The potter takes the clay thus abandoned to his working and begins to mold and fashion it according to his own will. He kneads and works it; he tears it apart and presses it together again; he wets it and then suffers it to dry. Sometimes he works at it for hours together; sometimes he lays it aside for days and does not touch it. And then, when by all these processes he has made it perfectly pliable in his hands, he proceeds to make it up into the vessel he has proposed. He turns it upon the wheel, planes it, and smoothes it, and dries it in the sun, bakes it in the oven, and finally turns it out of his workshop, a vessel to his honor, and fit for his use."

Will my reader be likely now to say that I am contradicting myself, that a little while ago I had said the clay had nothing to do but to lie passive in the potter's hands, and that now I am putting upon it a great work, which it is not able to perform, and that to make itself into such a vessel is an impossible and hopeless undertaking? Surely not. For he will see that while before I was speaking of the clay's part in the matter, I am now speaking of the potter's part, and that these two are necessarily contrasted, but not in the least contradictory; and that the clay is not expected to do the potter's work, but only to yield itself up to his working.

Nothing, it seems to me, could be clearer than the perfect harmony between these two *apparently* contradictory sorts of teaching.

What *can* be said about man's part in this great work but that he must continually surrender himself and continually trust? But when we come to God's side of the question, what is there that may not be said as to the manifold and wonderful ways in which He accomplishes the work entrusted to Him? It is here that the growing comes in. The lump of clay could never grow into a beautiful vessel if it stayed in the clay-pit for thousands of years; but when it is put into the hands of a skillful potter it grows rapidly, under his fashioning, into the vessel he intends it to be.

And in the same way the soul, abandoned to the working of the Heavenly Potter, is made into a vessel unto honor, sanctified and meet for the Master's use.

Having, therefore, taken the step of faith by which you have put yourself wholly and absolutely into His hands, you must now expect Him to begin to work. His way of accomplishing that which you have entrusted to Him may be different from your way; but He knows, and you must be satisfied.

I knew a lady who had entered into this life of faith with a great outpouring of the Spirit and a wonderful flood of light and joy. She supposed, of course, this was a preparation for some great service and expected to be put forth immediately into the Lord's harvestfield. Instead of this, almost at once her own husband lost all his money, and she was shut up in her own house to attend to all sorts of domestic duties with no time or strength left for any gospel work at all. She accepted the discipline and yielded herself up as heartily to sweep and dust and bake and sew, as she would have done to preach or pray or write for the Lord. And the result was that, through this very training, He made her into a vessel "meet for the master's use, and prepared unto every good work."

Another lady, who had entered this life of faith under similar circumstances of wondrous blessing and who also expected to be sent out to do some great work, was shut up with two peevish invalid children, to nurse and humor and amuse all day long. Unlike the first one, this lady did not accept the training but chafed and fretted and finally rebelled, lost all her blessing, and went back into a state of sad coldness and misery. She had understood her part of trusting to begin with, but, not understanding the divine process of accomplishing that for which she had trusted, she took herself out of the hands of the Heavenly Potter, and the vessel was marred on the wheel.

I believe many a vessel has been similarly marred by a want of understanding these things. The maturity of a Christian experience cannot be reached in a moment but is the result of the work of God's Holy Spirit, who, by His energizing and transforming power, causes us to grow up into Christ in all things. And we cannot hope to reach this maturity in any other way than by yielding ourselves up, utterly and willingly, to His mighty working. But the sanctification the scriptures urge as a present experience upon all believers does not consist in maturity of growth but in purity of heart; and this may be as complete in the early, as in our later experiences.

The lump of clay, from the moment it comes under the transforming hand of the potter is during each day and each hour of the process just what the potter wants it to be at that hour or on that day and therefore pleases him; but it is very far from being matured into the vessel he intends in the future to make it.

The little babe may be all that a babe could be, or ought to be, and may therefore perfectly please its mother; and yet it is very far from being what that mother would wish it to be when the years of maturity shall come.

The apple in June is a perfect apple for June; it is the best apple that June can produce: but it is very different from the apple in October, which is a perfected apple.

God's works are perfect in every stage of their growth. Man's works are never perfect until they are in every respect complete.

All that we claim, then, in this life of sanctification is that by an act of faith we put ourselves into the hands of the Lord, for Him to work in us all the good pleasure of His will, and then, by a continuous exercise of faith, keep ourselves there. This is our part in the matter. And when we do it, and while we do it, we are, in the scripture sense, truly pleasing God, although it may require years of training and discipline to mature us into a vessel that shall be in all respects to His honor and fitted to every good work.

Our part is the trusting; it is His to accomplish the results. And when we do our part, He never fails to do His, for no one ever trusted in the Lord and was confounded. Do not be afraid, then, that if you trust or tell others to trust, the matter will end there. Trust is the beginning and the continuing foundation; but when we trust, the Lord works, and His work is the important part of the whole matter. And this explains that apparent paradox which puzzles so many. They say, "In one breath you tell us to do nothing but trust, and in the next you tell us to do impossible things.

"How can you reconcile such contradictory statements?" They are to be reconciled, just as we reconcile the statements concerning a saw in a carpenter's shop, when we say, at one moment, that the saw has sawn asunder a log, and the next moment declare that the carpenter has done it. The saw is the instrument used; the power that uses it is the carpenter's. And so we, yielding ourselves unto God, and our members as instruments of righteousness unto Him, find that He works in us to will and to do of His good pleasure, and we can say with Paul, "I laboured. . .yet not I, but the grace of God which was with me."

In the divine order, God's working depends upon our cooperation. Of our Lord it was declared that at a certain place He could do there no mighty work because of their unbelief. It was not that He would not, but He could not. I believe we often think of God that He will not, when the real truth is that He cannot. Just as the potter, however skillful, cannot make a beautiful vessel out of a lump of clay that is never put into his hands, so neither can God make out of me a vessel unto His honor unless I put myself into

His hands. My part is the essential correlation of God's part in the matter of my salvation; and as God is *sure* to do His part all right, the vital thing for me is to find out what my part is and then do it.

In this book, therefore, I shall of course dwell mostly upon man's side, as I am writing for human beings, and in the hope of making it plain how we are to fulfill our part of this great work. But I wish it to be distinctly understood all through, that unless I believed with all my heart in God's effectual working on His side, not one word of this book would ever have been written.

Chapter 3

The Life Defined

I n the first chapter I have tried to settle the question as to the scripturalness of the experience sometimes called the Higher Christian Life but which is the only true Christian life and which to my own mind is best described in the words, the "life hid with Christ in God." In the second, I have sought to reconcile the two distinct sides of this life; that is, the part to be done by the Lord and the part necessarily to be done by ourselves. I shall now, therefore, consider it as a settled point that the scriptures do set before the believer in the Lord Jesus a life of abiding rest and of continual victory, which is very far beyond the ordinary run of Christian experience; and that in the Bible we have presented to us a Savior able to save us from the power of our sins as really as He saves us from their guilt.

The point to be next considered is as to what are the chief characteristics of this life hid with Christ in God and how it differs from much in the ordinary Christian experience.

Its chief characteristics are an entire surrender to the Lord and a perfect trust in Him, resulting in victory over sin and inward rest of soul; and it differs from the lower range of Christian experience in that it causes us to let the Lord carry our burdens and manage our affairs for us instead of trying to do it ourselves.

Most Christians are like a man who was toiling along the road, bending under a heavy burden, when a wagon overtook him, and the driver kindly offered to help him on his journey. He joyfully accepted the offer but, when seated in the wagon, continued to bend beneath his burden, which he still kept on his shoulders. "Why do you not lay down your burden?" asked the kind-hearted driver. "Oh!" replied the man, "I feel that it is almost too much to ask you to carry me, and I could not think of letting you carry my burden, too." And so Christians, who have given themselves into the care and keeping of the Lord Jesus, still continue to bend beneath the weight of their burdens and often go weary and heavy laden throughout the whole length of their journey.

When I speak of burdens, I mean everything that troubles us, whether spiritual or temporal.

I mean, first of all, ourselves. The greatest burden we have to carry in life is self; the most difficult thing we have to manage is self. Our own daily living, our frames and feelings, our special weaknesses and temptations, our peculiar temperaments, our inward affairs of every kind—these are the things that perplex and worry us more than anything else and that bring us most frequently into bondage and darkness. In laying off your burdens, therefore, the first one you must get rid of is yourself. You must hand yourself, with your temptations, your temperament, your frames and feelings, and all your inward and outward experiences, over into the care and keeping of your God and leave it all there.

He made you and, therefore, He understands you and knows how to manage you; you must trust Him to do it. Say to Him, "Here, Lord, I abandon myself to Thee. I have tried in every way I could think of to manage myself, and to make myself what I know I ought to be but have always failed. Now I give it up to Thee. Do Thou take entire possession of me. Work in me all the good pleasure of Thy will. Mold and fashion me into such a vessel as seemeth good to Thee. I leave myself in Thy hands, and I believe Thou wilt, according to Thy promise, make me into a vessel unto Thy own honor, 'sanctified, and meet for the master's use, and prepared unto every good work.' " And here you must rest, trusting yourself thus to Him, continually and absolutely.

Next, you must lay off every other burden—your health, your reputation, your Christian work, your houses, your children, your business, your servants; everything, in short, that concerns you, whether inward or outward.

It is generally much less difficult for us to commit the keeping of our future to the Lord than it is to commit our present. We know we are helpless as regards the future, but we feel as if the present was in our own hands and must be carried on our own shoulders; and most of us have an unconfessed idea that it is a great deal to ask the Lord to carry ourselves, and that we cannot think of asking Him to carry our burdens, too.

I knew a Christian lady who had a very heavy temporal burden. It took away her sleep and her appetite, and there was danger of her health breaking down under it. One day, when it seemed specially heavy, she noticed lying on the table near her a little tract called "Hannah's Faith." Attracted by the title, she picked it up and began to read it, little knowing, however, that it was to create a revolution in her whole experience. The story was of a poor woman who had been carried triumphantly through a life of unusual sorrow. She was giving the history of her life to a kind visitor on one occasion, and at the close the visitor said feelingly, "Oh, Hannah, I do not see how you could bear so much sorrow!" "I did not bear it," was the quick reply; "the Lord bore it for me." "Yes," said the visitor, "that is the right way. We must take our troubles to the Lord." "Yes," replied Hannah, "but we must do more than that: we must *leave* them there. Most people," she continued, "take their burdens to Him, but they bring them away with them again and are just as worried and unhappy as ever. But I take mine, and I leave them with Him and come away and forget them. If the worry comes back, I take it to Him again; and I do this over and over until at last I just forget I have any worries and am at perfect rest."

My friend was very much struck with this plan and resolved to try it. The circumstances of her life she could not alter, but she took them to the Lord and handed them over into His management; and then she believed that He took it, and she left all the responsibility and the worry and anxiety with Him. As often as the anxieties returned, she took them back, and the result was that, although the circumstances remained unchanged, her soul was kept in perfect peace in the midst of them. She felt that she had found out a practical secret; and from that time she sought never to carry her own burdens, nor to manage her own affairs, but to hand them over, as fast as they arose, to the Divine Burden-Bearer.

This same secret, also, which she had found to be so effectual in her outward life, proved to be still more effectual in her inward life, which was in truth even more utterly unmanageable. She abandoned her whole self to the Lord, with all that she was and all that she had, and, believing that He took that which she had committed to Him, she ceased to fret and worry, and her life became all sunshine in the gladness of belonging to Him. It was a very simple secret she found out; only this, that it was possible to obey God's commandment contained in those words, "Be careful for nothing; but in every thing by prayer and supplication with thanksgiving let your requests be made known unto God";

and that in obeying it, the result would inevitably be, according to the promise, that the "peace of God, which passeth all understanding, shall keep your hearts and minds through Christ Jesus."

There are many other things to be said about this life hid with Christ in God, many details as to what the Lord Jesus does for those who thus abandon themselves to Him. But the gist of the whole matter is here stated; and the soul that has discovered this secret of simple faith has found the key that will unlock the whole treasure-house of God.

I am sure these pages will fall into the hands of some child of God who is hungering for just such a life as I have been describing. You long unspeakably to get rid of your weary burdens. You would be delighted to hand over the management of your unmanageable self into the hands of one who is able to manage you. You are tired and weary, and the rest I speak of looks unutterably sweet to you.

Do you recollect the delicious sense of rest with which you have sometimes gone to bed at night, after a day of great exertion and weariness? How delightful was the sensation of relaxing every muscle and letting your body go in a perfect abandonment of ease and comfort! The strain of the day had ceased, for a few hours at least, and the work of the day had been laid off. You no longer had to hold up an aching head or a weary back. You trusted yourself to the bed in an absolute confidence, and it held you up, without effort or strain or even thought, on your part. You rested!

But suppose you had doubted the strength or the stability of your bed and had dreaded each moment to find it giving way beneath you and landing you on the floor; could you have rested then? Would not every muscle have been strained in a fruitless effort to hold yourself up, and would not the weariness have been greater than if you had not gone to bed at all?

Let this analogy teach you what it means to rest in the Lord. Let your souls lie down upon the couch of His sweet will, as your bodies lie down in their beds at night. Relax every strain, and lay off every burden. Let yourself go in a perfect abandonment of ease and comfort, sure that, since He holds you up, you are perfectly safe. Your part is simply to rest. His part is to sustain you; and He cannot fail.

Or take another analogy, which our Lord Himself has abundantly sanctioned—that of the child-life. For "Jesus called a little child unto him, and set him in the midst of them, and said. . . , Except ye be converted, and become as little children, ye shall not enter into the kingdom of heaven."

Now what are the characteristics of a little child, and how does he live? He lives by faith, and his chief characteristic is freedom from care. His life is one long trust from year's end to year's end. He trusts his parents, he trusts his caretakers, he trusts his teachers; he even trusts people sometimes who are utterly unworthy of trust, out of the abounding trustfulness of his nature. And this trust is abundantly answered. The child provides nothing for himself, and yet everything is provided. He takes no thought for the morrow and forms no plans, and yet all his life is planned out for him, and he finds his paths made ready, opening out as he comes to them day by day and hour by hour. He goes in and out of his father's house with an unspeakable ease and abandonment, enjoying all the good things therein, without having spent a penny in procuring them. Pestilence may walk through the streets of his city, but the child regards it not. Famines and fire and war may rage around him, but under his father's tender care the child abides in utter unconcern and perfect rest. He lives in the present moment and receives his life unquestioningly, as it comes to him day by day from his father's hand.

I was visiting once in a wealthy home where there was a little adopted child upon whom was lavished all the love and tenderness and care that human hearts could bestow or human means procure. And as I watched that child running in and out day by day, free and lighthearted with the happy carelessness of childhood, I thought what a picture it was of our wonderful position as children in the house of our heavenly Father. And I said to myself, *If nothing would so grieve and wound the loving hearts around her, as to see this little child beginning to be worried or anxious about herself in any way—about whether her food and clothes would be provided, or how she was to get her education or her future support—how much more must the great, loving heart of our God and Father be grieved and wounded at seeing His children taking so much anxious care and thought!* And I understood why it was that our Lord had said to us so emphatically, "Take no thought for yourselves."

Who is the best cared for in every household? Is it not the little children? And does not the least of all, the helpless baby, receive the largest share? We all know that the baby toils not, neither does he spin; and yet he is fed and clothed and loved and rejoiced in more tenderly than the hardest worker of them all.

This life of faith, then, about which I am writing consists in just this—being a child in the Father's house. And when this is said, enough is said to transform every weary, burdened life into one of blessedness and rest.

Let the ways of childish confidence and freedom from care, which so please you and win your hearts in your own little ones, teach you what should be your ways with God; and, leaving yourselves in His hands, learn to be literally "careful for nothing"; and you shall find it to be a fact that the peace of God, which passeth all understanding, shall keep (as with a garrison) your hearts and minds through Christ Jesus.

"Thou wilt keep him in perfect peace, whose mind is

stayed on thee: because he trusteth in thee." This is the divine description of the life of faith about which I am writing. It is no speculative theory; neither is it a dream of romance. There *is* such a thing as having one's soul kept in perfect peace, now and here in this life; and childlike trust in God is the key to its attainment.

Chapter 4

How to Enter In

Having sought to settle the question as to the scripturalness of an actual living of this life hid with Christ in
God, and having also shown a little of what it is, the next point
is as to how it is to be reached and realized.

I would say, first of all, that this blessed life must not be
looked upon in any sense as an attainment but as an obtain-
ment. We cannot earn it; we cannot climb up to it; we cannot win it; we can do nothing but ask for it and receive it. It
is the gift of God in Christ Jesus. And where a thing is a gift,
the only course left for the receiver is to take it and thank the
giver. We never say of a gift, "See to what I have attained,"
and boast of our skill and wisdom in having attained it; but
we say, "See what has been given to me," and boast of the
love and wealth and generosity of the giver. And everything
in our salvation is a gift. From beginning to end, God is the
giver, and we are the receivers; and it is not to those who do
great things but to those who "receive abundance of grace
and of the gift of righteousness," that the richest promises
are made.

In order, therefore, to enter into a practical experience of
this interior life, the soul must be in a receptive attitude,

43

fully recognizing the fact that it is God's gift in Christ Jesus, and that it cannot be gained by any efforts or works of our own. This will simplify the matter exceedingly; and the only thing left to be considered then, will be to discover upon whom God bestows this gift and how they are to receive it. To this I would answer, in short, that He can bestow it only upon the fully consecrated soul, and that it is to be received by faith.

Consecration is the first thing—not in any legal sense, not in order to purchase or deserve the blessing but to remove the difficulties out of the way and make it possible for God to bestow it. In order for a lump of clay to be made into a beautiful vessel, it must be entirely abandoned to the potter and must lie passive in his hands. And similarly, in order for a soul to be made into a vessel unto God's honor, "sanctified, and meet for the master's use, and prepared unto every good work," it must be utterly abandoned to Him, and must lie passive in His hands. This is manifest at the first glance.

I was once trying to explain to a physician, who had charge of a large hospital, the necessity and meaning of consecration, but he seemed unable to understand. At last I said to him, "Suppose, in going your rounds among your patients, you should meet with one man who entreated you earnestly to take his case under your special care in order to cure him, but who should at the same time refuse to tell you all his symptoms or to take all your prescribed remedies, and should say to you, 'I am quite willing to follow your directions as to certain things, because they commend themselves to my mind as good, but in other matters I prefer judging for myself and following my own directions.' What would you do in such a case?" I asked. "Do!" he replied with indignation—"Do! I would soon leave such a man as that to his own care. For, of course," he added, "I could do nothing for him unless he would put his whole case into my hands without any reserves and would obey my directions implicitly."

"It is necessary, then," I said, "for doctors to be obeyed, if they are to have any chance to cure their patient?" *"Implicitly obeyed!"* was his emphatic reply. "And that is consecration," I continued. "God must have the whole case put into His hands without any reserves, and His directions must be implicitly followed." "I see it," he exclaimed. "I see it! And I will do it. God shall have His own way with me from henceforth."

To some minds perhaps the word "abandonment" might express this idea better than the word "consecration." But whatever word we use, we mean an entire surrender of the whole being to God—spirit, soul, and body placed under His absolute control, for Him to do with us just what He pleases. We mean that the language of our hearts, under all circumstances and in view of every act, is to be "Thy will be done." We mean the giving up of all liberty of choice. We mean a life of inevitable obedience.

To a soul ignorant of God, this may look hard; but to those who know Him, it is the happiest and most restful of lives. He is our Father, and He loves us, and He knows just what is best, and therefore, of course, His will is the very most blessed thing that can come to us under any circumstances. I do not understand how it is that the eyes of so many Christians have been blinded to this fact. But it really would seem as if God's own children were more afraid of His will than of anything else in life—His lovely, lovable will, which only means loving-kindnesses and tender mercies and blessings unspeakable to their souls! I wish I could only show to every one the unfathomable sweetness of the will of God. Heaven is a place of infinite bliss because His will is perfectly done there, and our lives share in this bliss just in proportion as His will is perfectly done in them. He loves us—*loves us,* I say—and the will of love is always blessing for its loved one. Some of us know what it is to love, and we know that could we only have our way, our beloved ones would be overwhelmed with blessings. All that is good and sweet and lovely in life would be poured out upon them from our lavish hands, had we but the power to carry out our will for them. And if this is the way of love with us, how much more must it be so with our God, who is love itself! Could we but for one moment get a glimpse into the mighty depths of His love, our hearts would spring out to meet His will and embrace it as our richest treasure; and we would abandon ourselves to it with an enthusiasm of gratitude and joy, that such a wondrous privilege could be ours.

A great many Christians seem practically to think that all their Father in heaven wants is a chance to make them miserable and to take away all their blessings; and they imagine, poor souls, that if they hold on to things in their own will, they can hinder Him from doing this. I am ashamed to write the words, yet we must face a fact which is making wretched hundreds of lives.

A Christian who was in a great deal of trouble was recounting to another Christian the various efforts he had made to find deliverance and concluded by saying, "But it has all been in vain, and there is literally nothing left for me to do but to trust the Lord."

"Alas!" exclaimed his friend in a tone of the deepest commiseration, as though no greater risk were possible—"Alas! Has it come to *that*?"

A Christian lady who had this feeling was once expressing to a friend how impossible she found it to say, "Thy will be done," and how afraid she should be to do it. She was the mother of an only little boy, who was the heir to a great fortune and the idol of her heart. After she had stated her difficulties fully, her friend said, "Suppose your little Charley should come running to you tomorrow and say, 'Mother, I have made up my mind to let you have your own way with me from this time forward. I am always going to obey you, and I want you to do just whatever you think best with me. I will trust your love.' How would you feel toward him? Would you say to yourself, 'Ah, now I shall have a chance to make Charley miserable. I will take away all his pleasures and fill his life with every hard and disagreeable thing that I can find. I will compel him to do just the things that are the most difficult for him to do and will give him all sorts of impossible commands.' " "Oh, no, no, no!" exclaimed the indignant mother. "You know I would not. You know I would hug him to my heart and cover him with kisses and would hasten to fill his life with all that was sweetest and best." "And are you more tender and more loving than God?" asked her friend. "Ah, no!" was the reply. "I see my mistake. Of course I must not be any more afraid of saying, 'Thy will be done,' to my heavenly Father, than I would want Charley to be of saying it to me."

Better and sweeter than health or friends or money or fame or ease or prosperity is the adorable will of our God. It gilds the darkest hours with a divine halo and sheds brightest sunshine on the gloomiest paths. He always reigns who has made it his kingdom, and nothing can go amiss to him. Surely, then, it is only a glorious privilege that is opening before you, when I tell you that the first step you must take in order to enter into the life hid with Christ in God, is that of entire consecration. I beg of you not to look at it as a hard and stern demand. You must do it gladly, thankfully, enthusiastically. You must go in on what I call the privilege side of consecration; and I can assure you from the universal testimony of all who have tried it, that you will find it the happiest place you have ever entered yet.

Faith is the next thing after surrender. Faith is an absolutely necessary element in the reception of any gift; for let our friends give a thing to us ever so fully, it is not really ours until we believe it has been given and claim it as our own. Above all, this is true in gifts which are purely mental or spiritual. Love may be lavished upon us by another without stint or measure, but until we believe that we are loved, it never really becomes ours.

I suppose most Christians understand this principle in reference to the matter of their forgiveness. They know that the forgiveness of sins through Jesus might have been preached to them forever, but it would never really have become theirs until they believed this preaching and claimed the forgiveness as their own. But when it comes to living the Christian life, they lose sight of this principle and think that, having been saved by faith, they are now to live by works and efforts; and instead of continuing to *receive*, they are now to begin to *do*. This makes our declaration that the life hid with Christ in God is to be entered by faith seem perfectly unintelligible to them. And yet it is plainly declared, that, "*as* ye have therefore received Christ Jesus the Lord, *so* walk ye in Him." We received Him by faith, and by faith alone; therefore, we are to walk in Him by faith and by faith alone. And the faith by which we enter into this hidden life is just the same as the faith by which we were translated out of the kingdom of darkness into the kingdom of God's dear Son, only it lays hold of a different thing. *Then* we believed that Jesus was our Savior from the guilt of sin, and according to our faith it was unto us; *now* we must believe that He is our Savior from the power of sin, and according to our faith it shall be unto us. *Then* we trusted Him for forgiveness, and it became ours; *now* we must trust Him for righteousness, and it shall become ours also. *Then* we took Him as a Savior in the future from the penalties of our sins; *now* we must take Him as a Savior in the present from the bondage of our sins. *Then* He was our Redeemer; *now* He is to be our Life.

Then He lifted us out of the pit; *now* He is to seat us in heavenly places with Himself.

I mean all this, of course, experimentally and practically. Theologically and judicially I know that every believer has everything as soon as he is converted; but experimentally nothing is his until by faith he claims it. "Every place that the sole of your foot shall tread upon, that have I given unto you." God "hath blessed us with all spiritual blessings in heavenly places in Christ"; but until we set the foot of faith upon them, they do not practically become ours. "According to our faith" is always the limit and the rule.

But this faith of which I am speaking must be a present faith. No faith that is exercised in the future tense amounts to anything. A man may believe forever that his sins will be forgiven at some future time, and he will never find peace. He has to come to the *now* belief and say by a present appropriating faith, "My sins are now forgiven," before his soul can be at rest. And similarly, no faith that looks for a future deliverance from the power of sin will ever lead a soul into the life we are describing. The enemy delights in this future faith, for he knows it is powerless to accomplish any practical results. But he trembles and flees when the soul of the believer dares to claim a present deliverance and to reckon itself *now* to be free from his power.

Perhaps no four words in the language have more meaning in them than the following, which I would have you repeat over and over with your voice and with your soul, emphasizing each time a different word:

Jesus saves me now—It is He.

Jesus *saves* me now—It is His work to save.

Jesus saves *me* now—I am the one to be saved.

Jesus saves me *now*—He is doing it every moment.

To sum up, then: In order to enter into this blessed interior life of rest and triumph, you have two steps to take—first, entire abandonment; and second, absolute faith. No matter what may be the complications of your peculiar experience, no matter what your difficulties or your surroundings or your "peculiar temperament," these two steps, definitely taken and unwaveringly persevered in, will certainly bring you out sooner or later into the green pastures and still waters of this life hid with Christ in God. You may be perfectly sure of this. And if you will let every other consideration go and simply devote your attention to these two points and be very clear and definite about them, your progress will be rapid, and your soul will reach its desired haven far sooner than you can now think possible.

Shall I repeat the steps, that there may be no mistakes? You are a child of God and long to please Him. You love your divine master and are sick and weary of the sin that grieves Him. You long to be delivered from its power. Everything you have hitherto tried has failed to deliver you; and now, in your despair, you are asking if it can indeed be, as these happy people say, that Jesus is able and willing to deliver you. Surely you must know in your very soul that He is—that to save you out of the hand of all your enemies is, in fact, just the very thing He came to do. Then trust Him. Commit your case to Him in an absolute unreserve, and believe that He undertakes it; and at once, knowing what He is and what He has said, claim that He does even now save you. Just as you believed at first that He delivered you from the guilt of sin because He said it, so now believe that He delivers you from the power of sin because He says it.

Let your faith now lay hold of a new power in Christ. You have trusted Him as your dying Savior; now trust Him as your living Savior. Just as much as He came to deliver you from future punishment, did He also come to deliver you from present bondage. Just as truly as He came to bear your stripes for you, has He come to live your life for you. You are as utterly powerless in the one case as in the other. You could as easily have got yourself rid of your own sins as you could now accomplish for yourself practical righteousness. Christ, and Christ only, must do both for you; and your part in both cases is simply to give the thing to Him to do and then believe that He does it.

A lady, now very eminent in this life of trust, when she was seeking in great darkness and perplexity to enter in, said to the friend who was trying to help her, "You all say, 'Abandon yourself and trust, abandon yourself and trust'; but I do not know how. I wish you would just do it out loud, so that I may see how you do it."

Shall I do it out loud for you?

"Lord, Jesus, I believe that Thou art able and willing to deliver me from all the care and unrest and bondage of my Christian life. I believe Thou didst die to set me free, not only in the future, but now and here. I believe Thou art stronger than sin, and that Thou canst keep me, even me, in my extreme of weakness, from falling into its snares or yielding obedience to its commands. And, Lord, I am going to trust Thee to keep me. I have tried keeping myself and have failed, and failed most grievously. I am absolutely helpless. So now I will trust Thee. I give myself to Thee. I keep back no reserves. Body, soul, and spirit, I present myself to Thee, as a piece of clay, to be fashioned into anything Thy love and Thy wisdom shall choose. And now I *am* Thine. I believe Thou dost accept that which I present to Thee; I believe that this poor, weak, foolish heart has been taken possession of by Thee, and that Thou hast even at this very moment begun to work in me to will and to do of Thy good pleasure. I trust Thee *utterly*, and I trust Thee *now*."

A man was obliged to descend into a deep well by sliding down a fixed rope which was supposed to be of ample length. But to his dismay he came to the end of it before his feet had touched the bottom. He had not the strength to climb up again and to let go and drop seemed to him but to be dashed to pieces in the depths below. He held on until his strength was utterly exhausted and then dropped, as he thought, to his death. He fell—just three inches—and found himself safe on the rock bottom.

Are you afraid to take this step? Does it seem too sudden, too much like a leap in the dark? Do you not know that the step of faith always "falls on the seeming void, but finds the rock beneath"? If ever you are to enter this glorious land, flowing with milk and honey, you must sooner or later step into the brimming waters, for there is no other path; and to do it now may save you months and even years of disappointment and grief. Hear the word of the Lord—

"Have not I commanded thee? Be strong and of good courage; be not afraid, neither be thou dismayed: for the LORD thy God is with thee withersoever thou goest."

PART II
DIFFICULTIES

Chapter 5

Difficulties Concerning Consecration

It is very important that Christians should not be ignorant of the temptations that seem to stand ready to oppose every onward step of their progress heavenward and that are especially active when the soul is awakened to a hunger and thirst after righteousness and begins to reach out after the fullness that is ours in Christ.

One of the greatest of these temptations is a difficulty concerning consecration. The seeker after holiness is told that he must consecrate himself, and he endeavors to do so. But at once he meets with a difficulty. He has done it as he thinks, and yet he finds no difference in his experience; nothing seems changed as he has been led to expect it would be, and he is completely baffled and asks the question almost despairingly, "How am I to know when I am consecrated?"

The one chief temptation that meets the soul at this juncture is the same that assaults it all along the pathway, at every step of its progress; namely, the question as to *feelings*. We cannot believe we are consecrated until we *feel* that we are; and because we do not feel that God has taken us in hand, we cannot believe that He has. As usual, we put feeling first and faith second and the fact last of all. Now

God's invariable rule in everything is fact first, faith second, and feeling last of all; and it is striving against the inevitable when we seek to change this order.

The way, then, to meet this temptation in reference to consecration is simply to take God's side in the matter and to adopt His order by putting faith before feeling. Give yourself to the Lord definitely and fully, according to your present light, asking the Holy Spirit to show you all that is contrary to Him, either in your heart or life. If He shows you anything, give it to the Lord immediately and say in reference to it, "Thy will be done." If He shows you nothing, then you must believe that there is nothing and must conclude that you have given Him all. Then recognize that it must be the fact, that, when you give yourself to God, He accepts you; and at once let your faith take hold of this fact. Begin to believe, and hold on to it steadfastly, that He has taken that which you have surrendered to Him. You positively must not wait to feel either that you have given yourself or that God has taken you. You must simply believe it and reckon it to be the case. And if you are steadfast in this reckoning, sooner or later the feeling will come, and you will realize that it is indeed a blessed fact that you are wholly the Lord's.

If you were to give an estate to a friend, you would have to give it, and he would have to receive it, by faith. An estate is not a thing that can be picked up and handed over to another; the gift of it and its reception are altogether a transaction by word and on paper, and therefore one of faith. Now, if you should give an estate one day to a friend, and then should go away and wonder whether you really had given it, and whether he actually had taken it and considered it his own, and should feel it necessary to go the next day and renew the gift; and if on the third day you should still feel a similar uncertainty about it, and should again go and renew the gift; and on the fourth day go through a like process, and so on, day after day, for months and years—what would your friend think, and what at last would be the condition of your own mind in reference to it? Your friend would certainly begin to doubt whether you ever had intended to give it to him at all, and you yourself would be in such hopeless perplexity about it that you would not know whether the estate was yours or his or whose it was.

Now, is not this very much the way in which you have been acting toward God in this matter of consecration? You have given yourself to Him over and over daily, perhaps for months, but you have invariably come away from your seasons of consecration wondering whether you really have given yourself after all and whether He has taken you; and because you have not *felt* any change, you have concluded at last, after many painful tossings, that the thing has not been done. Do you know, dear believer, that this sort of perplexity will last forever unless you cut it short by faith? You must come to the point of reckoning the matter to be an accomplished and settled thing and must leave it there before you can possibly expect any change of feeling whatever.

The Levitical law of offerings to the Lord settles this as a primary fact, that everything which is given to Him becomes, by that very act, something holy, set apart from all other things, something that cannot without sacrilege be put to any other uses. "Notwithstanding no devoted thing, that a man shall devote unto the LORD of all that he hath, both of man and beast, and of the field of his possession, shall be sold or redeemed: every devoted thing is most holy unto the LORD." Having once given it to the Lord, the devoted thing henceforth was reckoned by all Israel as being the Lord's, and no one dared to stretch forth a hand to retake it. The giver might have made his offering very grudgingly and half-heartedly, but, having made it, the matter was taken out of his hands altogether, and the devoted thing, by God's own law, became "most holy unto the LORD." It was not made holy by the state of mind of the giver but by the holiness of the divine receiver. "The altar sanctifies that gift"; and an offering, once laid upon the altar, from the moment belonged to the Lord.

I can imagine an offerer, after he had deposited a gift, beginning to search his heart as to his sincerity and honesty in doing it and coming back to the priest to say that he was afraid, after all, he had not given it rightly or had not been perfectly sincere in giving it. I feel sure the priest would have silenced him at once, saying, "As to how you gave your offering or what were your motives in giving it, I do not know. The facts are that you did give it, and that it is the Lord's, for every devoted thing is most holy unto Him. It is too late to recall the transaction now." And not only the priest, but all Israel, would have been aghast at the man, who, having once given his offering, should have reached out his hand to take it back. Yet, day after day, earnest-hearted Christians, with no thought of the sacrilege they are committing, are guilty in their own experience of a similar act, by giving themselves to the Lord in solemn consecration and then, through unbelief, taking back that which they have given.

Because God is not visibly present to the eye, it is difficult to feel that a transaction with Him is real. I suppose that if, when we made our acts of consecration, we could actually see Him present with us, we should feel it to be a very real thing and would realize that we had given our word to Him and could not dare to take it back, no matter how much we might wish to do so. Such a transaction would have to us the binding power that a spoken promise to an earthly friend always has to a man of honor. What we need, therefore, is to see that God's presence is a certain fact always, and that every act of our soul is done before Him, and that a word spoken in prayer is as really spoken to Him as if our eyes could see Him and our hands could touch Him. Then we shall cease to have such vague conceptions of our relations with Him and shall feel the binding force of every word we say in His presence.

I know some will say here, "Ah, yes; but if He would only speak to me and say that He took me when I gave myself to Him, I would have no trouble then in believing it." No, of course you would not; but then where would be the room for faith? Sight is not faith, and hearing is not faith, neither is feeling faith; but believing when we can neither see, hear, nor feel, *is* faith; and everywhere the Bible tells us our salvation is to be by faith. Therefore, we must believe before we feel, and often against our feelings, if we would honor God by our faith. It is always he that believeth who has the witness, not he that doubteth. But how can we doubt, since, by His very command to us to present ourselves to Him a living sacrifice, He has pledged Himself to receive us? I cannot conceive of an honorable man asking another to give him a thing which, after all, he was doubtful about taking; still less can I conceive of a loving parent acting so toward a beloved child. "My son, give me thy heart" is a sure warrant for knowing that the moment the heart is given, it will be taken by the one who has commanded the gift. We may, nay we must, feel the utmost confidence, then, that when we surrender ourselves to the Lord, according to His own command, He does then and there receive us, and from that moment we are His. A real transaction has taken place, which cannot be violated without dishonor on our part, and which we know will not be violated by Him.

In Deuteronomy 26:17–19, we see God's way of working under these circumstances. "Thou hast avouched the LORD this day to be thy God, and to walk in his ways, and to keep his statutes, and his commandments, and his judgments, and to hearken unto his voice: and the LORD hath avouched thee this day to be his peculiar people, as he hath promised thee, and that thou shouldest keep all his commandments. . .and that thou mayest be an holy people unto the LORD thy God, as he hath spoken."

When we avouch the Lord to be our God and that we will walk in His ways and keep His commandments, He avouches us to be His and that we *shall* keep all His commandments. And from that moment He takes possession of us. This has always been His principle of working, and it continues to be so. "Every devoted thing is most holy unto the LORD." This is so plain as not to admit of a question.

But if the soul still feels in doubt or difficulty, let me refer you to a New Testament declaration which approaches the subject from a different side, but which settles it, I think, quite as definitely. It is in 1 John 5:14–15, and reads, "And this is the confidence that we have in him, that, if we ask any thing according to his will, he heareth us: and if we know that he hear us, whatsoever we ask, we know that we have the petitions that we desired of him." Is it according to His will that you should be entirely surrendered to Him? There can be, of course, but one answer to this, for He has *commanded* it. Is it not also according to His will that He should work in you to will and to do of His good pleasure? This question also can have but one answer, for He has declared it to be His purpose. You know, then, that these things are according to His will; therefore, on God's own word, you are obliged to know that He hears you. And knowing this much, you are compelled to go farther and know that you have the petitions that you have desired of Him. That you *have,* I say—not will have, or may have, but have now in actual possession. It is thus that we "obtain promises" by faith. It is thus that we have "access by faith" into the grace that is given us in our Lord Jesus Christ. It is thus, and thus only, that we come to know our hearts "purified by faith," and are enabled to live by faith, to stand by faith, to walk by faith.

I desire to make this subject so plain and practical that no one need have any further difficulty about it and, therefore, I will repeat again just what must be the acts of your soul, in order to bring you out of this difficulty about consecration.

I suppose that you have trusted the Lord Jesus for the forgiveness of your sins and know something of what it is to belong to the family of God and to be made an heir of God through faith in Christ. And now you feel springing up in your heart the longing to be conformed to the image of your Lord. In order for this to happen, you know there must be an entire surrender of yourself to Him, that He may work in you all the good pleasure of His will; and you have tried over and over to do it but hitherto without any apparent success. At this point it is that I desire to help you. What you must do now is to come once more to Him, in a surrender of your whole self to His will, as complete as you know how to make it. You must ask Him to reveal to you, by His Spirit, any hidden rebellion; and if He reveals nothing, then you must believe that there is nothing, and that the surrender is complete. This must, then, be considered a settled matter; you have wholly yielded yourself to the Lord, and from henceforth you do not in any sense belong to yourself; you must never even so much as listen to a suggestion to the contrary. If the temptation comes to wonder whether you really have completely surrendered yourself, meet it with an assertion that you have. Do not even argue the matter. Repel any such idea instantly, and with decision. You meant it then; you mean it now; you have really done it. Your emotions may clamor against the surrender, but your will must hold firm. It is your purpose God looks at, not your feelings about that purpose; and your purpose, or will, is therefore the only thing you need to attend to.

The surrender, then, having been made, never to be questioned or recalled, the next point is to believe that God takes that which you have surrendered and to reckon that it is His. Not that it will be His at some future time, but that it is now; and that He has begun to work in you to will and to do of His good pleasure. And here you must rest. There is nothing more for you to do, except to be henceforth an obedient child; for you are the Lord's now, absolutely and entirely in His hands, and He has undertaken the whole care and management and forming of you, and will, according to his word, "work in you that which is well-pleasing in His sight through Jesus Christ." But you must hold steadily here. If you begin to question your surrender or God's acceptance of it, then your wavering faith will produce a wavering experience, and He cannot work in you to do His will. But while you trust, He works; and the result of His working always is to change you into the image of Christ, from glory to glory, by His mighty Spirit.

Do you, then, now at this moment, surrender yourself wholly to Him? You answer, Yes. Then, my dear friend, begin at once to reckon that you are His, that He has taken you, and that He is working in you to will and to do of His good pleasure. And keep on reckoning this. You will find it a great help to put your reckoning into words and say over and over to yourself and to your God, "Lord, I am Yours; I do yield myself up entirely to You, and I believe that You accept me. I leave myself with You. Work in me all the good pleasure of Your will, and I will only lie still in Your hands and trust You."

Make this a daily, definite act of your will, and many times a day recur to it, as being your continual attitude before the Lord. Confess it to yourself. Confess it to your

God. Confess it to your friends. Avouch the Lord to be your God, continually and unwaveringly, and declare your purpose of walking in His ways and keeping His statutes; and sooner or later, you will find in practical experience that He has avouched you to be one of His peculiar people and will enable you to keep all His commandments, and that you are being made into "a holy people unto the Lord, as He hath spoken."

> *For thou are making me, I thank thee, Sire.*
> *What thou hast done and doest, thou knowest well;*
> *And I will help thee: gently in thy fire*
> *I will lie burning; on thy potter's wheel*
> *I will whirl patient, though my brain should reel;*
> *Thy grace shall be enough my grief to quell,*
> *And growing strength perfect through weakness dire.*

Chapter 6

Difficulties Concerning Faith

The next step after consecration, in the soul's progress out of the wilderness of a failing Christian experience into the land that floweth with milk and honey, is that of faith. And here, as in the first step, the soul encounters at once certain forms of difficulty and hindrance.

The child of God, whose eyes have been opened to see the fullness there is in Jesus for him, and whose heart has been made hungry to appropriate that fullness, is met with the assertion, on the part of every teacher to whom he applies, that this fullness is only to be received by faith. But the subject of faith is involved in such a hopeless mystery to his mind that this assertion, instead of throwing light upon the way of entrance, only seems to make it more difficult and involved than ever.

"Of course it is to be by faith," he says, "for I know that everything in the Christian life is by faith. But that is just what makes it so hard, for I have no faith, and I do not even know what it is, nor how to get it." And, thus, baffled at the very outset by this insuperable difficulty, he is plunged into darkness and almost despair.

This trouble arises from the fact that the subject of faith

is very generally misunderstood; for, in reality, faith is the simplest and plainest thing in the world and the most easy of exercise.

Your idea of faith, I suppose, has been something like this. You have looked upon it as in some way a sort of *thing* —either a religious exercise of soul, or an inward, gracious disposition of heart; something tangible, in fact, which, when you have secured it, you can look at and rejoice over and use as a passport to God's favor or a coin with which to purchase His gifts. And you have been praying for faith, expecting all the while to get something like this; and never having received any such thing, you are insisting upon it that you have no faith. Now faith, in fact, is not the least like this. It is nothing at all tangible. It is simply believing God; and, like your sight, it is nothing apart from its object. You might as well shut your eyes and look inside and see whether you have sight as to look inside to discover whether you have faith.

You see something and thus know that you have sight; you believe something and thus know that you have faith. For as sight is only seeing, so faith is only believing. And as the only necessary thing about sight is that you see the thing as it is, so the only necessary thing about belief is that you believe the thing as it is. The virtue does not lie in your believing but in the thing you believe. If you believe the truth, you are saved; if you believe a lie, you are lost. The act of believing in both cases is the same; the things believed are exactly opposite, and this it is which makes the mighty difference. Your salvation comes, not because your faith saves you, but because it links you to the Savior who saves; and your believing is really nothing but the link.

I do beg of you to recognize, then, the extreme simplicity of faith; namely, that it is nothing more nor less than just believing God when He says He either has done something for us, or will do it; and then trusting Him to keep His word. It is so simple that it is hard to explain. If any one asks me what it means to trust another to do a piece of work for me, I can only answer that it means committing the work to that other and leaving it without anxiety in his hands. All of us have many times trusted very important affairs to others in this way and have felt perfect rest in thus trusting because of the confidence we have had in those who have undertaken them.

How constantly do mothers trust their most precious infants to the care of nurses and feel no shadow of anxiety! How continually we are all of us trusting our health and our lives, without a thought of fear, to cooks and coachmen, engine drivers, railway conductors, and all sorts of paid servants, who have us completely at their mercy, and who could, if they chose to do so, or even if they failed in the necessary carefulness, plunge us into misery or death in a moment. All this we do and make no demur about it. Upon the slightest acquaintance, often, we thus put our trust in people, requiring only the general knowledge of human nature and the common rules of human intercourse as the foundation of our trust, and we never feel as if we were doing anything in the least remarkable.

You have done this yourself, dear reader, and are doing it continually. You could not live among your fellowmen and go through the customary routine of life a single day if you were unable to trust your fellowmen, and it never enters into your head to say you cannot. But yet you do not hesitate to say, continually, that you cannot trust your God! And you excuse yourself by the plea that you are "a poor weak creature" and "have no faith."

I wish you would try to imagine yourself acting in your human relations as you do in your spiritual relations. Suppose you should begin tomorrow with the notion in your head that you could not trust anybody because you had no faith. When you sat down to breakfast you would say, "I cannot eat anything on this table, for I have no faith, and I cannot believe the cook has not put poison into the coffee, or that the butcher has not sent home diseased or unhealthy meat," so you would go starving away. When you went out to your daily avocations, you would say, "I cannot ride in the railway train, for I have no faith, and therefore I cannot trust the engineer, nor the conductor, nor the builders of the carriages, nor the managers of the road." And you would be compelled to walk everywhere and would grow unutterably weary in the effort, besides being actually unable to reach the places you could have reached in the train.

When your friends met you with any statements or your business agent with any accounts, you would say, "I am very sorry that I cannot believe you, but I have no faith and never can believe anybody." If you opened a newspaper, you would be forced to lay it down again, saying, "I really cannot believe a word this paper says, for I have no faith; I do not believe there is any such person as the Queen, for I never saw her; nor any such country as Ireland, for I was never there. I have no faith, so of course I cannot believe anything that I have not actually felt and touched myself. It is a great trial, but I cannot help it, for I have no faith."

Just picture such a day as this and see how disastrous it would be to yourself and what utter folly it would appear to any one who should watch you through the whole of it. Realize how your friends would feel insulted and how your servants would refuse to serve you another day. And then ask yourself the question, if this want of faith in your fellowmen would be so dreadful and such utter folly, what must it be when you tell God that you have no power to trust Him, nor to believe His word; that it is a great trial, but you cannot help it, "for you have no faith."

Is it possible that you can trust your fellowmen and cannot trust your God; that you can receive the "witness of men" and cannot receive the "witness of God"; that you can believe man's records and cannot believe God's record; that you can commit your dearest earthly interests to your weak, failing fellow creatures without a fear and are afraid to commit your spiritual interests to the Savior who laid down His life for you and of whom it is declared that He is "able also to save them to the uttermost that come unto God by him"?

Surely, surely, dear believer, you, whose very name of believer implies that you can believe, you will never again dare to excuse yourself on the plea of having no faith. For when you say this, you mean, of course, that you have no faith in God since you are not asked to have faith in yourself and would be in a very wrong condition of soul if you had. Let me beg of you, then, when you think or say these things, always to complete the sentence and say, "I have no faith in—God! I cannot believe—God!" and this I am sure will soon become so dreadful to you that you will not dare to continue it.

But, you say, I cannot believe without the Holy Spirit. Very well; will you conclude, then, that your want of faith is because of the failure of the Holy Spirit to do His work? For if it is, then surely you are not to blame and need feel no condemnation; and all exhortations to you to believe are useless.

But no! Do you not see, that, in taking up the position that you have no faith and cannot believe, you are not only "making God a liar," but you are also showing an utter want of confidence in the Holy Spirit.

For He is always ready to help our infirmities. We never have to wait for Him; He is always waiting for us. And I for my part have such absolute confidence in the Holy Ghost and in His being always ready to do His work, that I dare to say to every one of you, that you *can* believe now, at this very moment; and that if you do not, it is not the Spirit's fault, but your own. Put your will, then, over on the believing side. Say, "Lord, I will believe; I do believe," and continue to say it. Insist upon believing in the face of every suggestion of doubt that intrudes itself. Out of your very unbelief, throw yourself unreservedly on the word and promises of God, and dare to abandon yourself to the keeping and saving power of the Lord Jesus. If you have ever trusted a precious interest in the hands of an earthly friend, I entreat you, trust yourself and all your spiritual interest now in the hands of your heavenly friend, and never, *never, never* allow yourself to doubt again.

Remember always that there are two things which are more utterly incompatible even than oil and water, and these two are trust and worry. Would you call it trust if you should give something into the hands of a friend to attend to for you and then should spend your nights and days in anxious thought and worry as to whether it would be rightly and successfully done? And can you call it trust when you have given the saving and keeping of your soul into the hands of the Lord if day after day and night after night, you are spending hours of anxious thought and questionings about the matter?

When a believer really trusts anything, he ceases to worry about the thing he has trusted. And when he worries, it is a plain proof that he does not trust. Tested by this rule, how little real trust there is in the church of Christ! No wonder our Lord asked the pathetic question, "When the Son of man cometh, shall he find faith on the earth?" He will find plenty of work, a great deal of earnestness, and doubtless many consecrated hearts; but shall He find faith, the one thing He values more than all the rest? Every child of God, in his own case, will know how to answer this question.

Should the answer, for any of you, be a sorrowful No, let me entreat you to let this be the last time for such an answer; and if you have ever known anything of the trustworthiness of our Lord, may you henceforth set to your seal that He is true by the generous recklessness of your trust in Him!

I remember, very early in my Christian life, having every tender and loyal impulse within me stirred to the depths by an appeal I met within a volume of old sermons, to all who loved the Lord Jesus, that they should show to others how worthy He was of being trusted by the steadfastness of their own faith in Him. As I read the inspiring words, there came to me a sudden glimpse of the privilege and the glory of being called to walk in paths so dark that only an utter recklessness of trust would be possible!

"Ye have not passed this way heretofore," it may be; but today it is your happy privilege to prove, as never before, your loyal confidence in Jesus, by starting out with Him on a life and walk of faith, lived, moment by moment in absolute and childlike trust in Him.

You have trusted Him in a few things, and He has not failed you. Trust Him now for everything, and see if He does not do for you exceeding abundantly, above all that you could ever have asked or even thought, not according to your power or capacity, but according to His own mighty power, working in you all the good pleasure of His most blessed will.

It is not hard, you find, to trust the management of the universe and of all the outward creation to the Lord. Can your case then be so much more complex and difficult than these, that you need to be anxious or troubled about His management of you? Away with such unworthy doubtings! Take your stand on the power and trustworthiness of your God, and see how quickly all difficulties will vanish before a steadfast determination to believe. Trust in the dark, trust in the light, trust at night and trust in the morning, and you will find that the faith that may begin perhaps by a mighty effort will end, sooner or later, by becoming the easy and natural habit of the soul. It is a law of spiritual life that every act of trust makes the next act less difficult, until at length, if these acts are persisted in, trusting becomes, like breathing, the natural unconscious action of the redeemed soul.

You must therefore put your will into your believing. Your faith must not be a passive imbecility but an active energy. You may have to believe against every seeming; but no matter. Set your face like a flint to say, "I will believe, and I know I shall not be confounded." We are made "partakers of Christ if we hold the beginning of our faith steadfast unto the end." Hundreds fail just here. They have a little beginning of faith, but discouragements come, the "seemings" are all against it, their doubts clamor louder and louder, and at last they let them in; and when doubt comes in at the door, trust always flies out of the window.

We are told that all things are possible to God, and that all things are possible also to him that believeth. Faith has in times past "subdued kingdoms, wrought righteousness, obtained promises, stopped the mouths of lions, quenched the violence of fire, escaped the edge of the sword. . .waxed valiant in fight, turned to flight the armies of the aliens"; and faith can do it again. For our Lord Himself says unto us, "If ye have faith as a grain of mustard seed, ye shall say unto this mountain, Remove hence to yonder place; and it shall remove; and nothing shall be impossible unto you."

If you are a child of God at all, you must have at least as much faith as a grain of mustard seed and, therefore, you dare not say again that you "cannot trust because you have no faith." Say rather, "I can trust my Lord, and I will trust Him; and not all the powers of earth or hell shall be able to make me doubt my wonderful, glorious, faithful redeemer!"

> *Faith is sweetest of worships to Him, who so*
> *loves His unbearable splendors in darkness to*
> *hide; and to trust to thy word, dearest Lord! is*
> *true love, for those prayers are most granted which*
> *seem most denied.*
>
> *Our faith throws her arms around all thou hast*
> *told her, and, able to hold as much more, can but*
> *grieve. She could hold thy grand self,*
> *Lord! if thou wouldst reveal it, and love makes*
> *her long to have more to believe.*

Let your faith then, "throw its arms around all God has told you," and in every dark hour remember that "though now for a season, if need be, ye are in heaviness through manifold temptations," it is only like going through a tunnel. The sun has not ceased shining because the traveler through the tunnel has ceased to see it; and the sun of righteousness is still shining, although you in your dark tunnel do not see Him. Be patient and trustful, and wait. This time of darkness is only permitted that "the trial of your faith, being much more precious than of gold that perisheth, though it be tried with fire, might be found unto praise and honour and glory at the appearing of Jesus Christ."

Chapter 7

Difficulties Concerning the Will

When the child of God has, by entire abandonment and absolute trust, stepped out of himself into Christ and has begun to know something of the blessedness of the life hid with Christ in God, there is one form of difficulty which is especially likely to start up in his path. After the first emotions of peace and rest have somewhat subsided, or if, as is sometimes the case, they have never seemed to come at all, he begins to feel such an utter unreality in the things he has been passing through that he seems to himself like a hypocrite when he says or even thinks they are real. It seems to him that his belief does not go below the surface; that it is a mere lip-belief and, therefore, of no account, and that his surrender is not a surrender of the heart and, therefore, cannot be acceptable to God. He is afraid to say he is altogether the Lord's, for fear he will be telling an untruth; and yet he cannot bring himself to say he is not, because he longs for it so intensely. The difficulty is real and very disheartening.

But there is nothing here which will not be very easily overcome when the Christian once thoroughly understands the principles of the new life and has learned *how* to live in it. The common thought is that this life hid with Christ in

God is to be lived in the emotions, and consequently all the attention of the soul is directed toward them, and as they are satisfactory or otherwise, the soul rests or is troubled. Now the truth is that this life is not to be lived in the emotions at all but in the will; and therefore, if only the will is kept steadfastly abiding in its center, God's will, the varying states of emotion do not in the least disturb or affect the reality of the life.

To make this plain, I must enlarge a little. Fenelon says, somewhere, that "pure religion resides in the will alone." By this he means that, as the will is the governing power in the man's nature, if the will is set right, all the rest of the nature must come into harmony. By the will, I do not mean the wish of the man or even his purpose but the deliberate choice, the deciding power, the king, to which all that is in the man must yield obedience. It is the man, in short, the *ego,* that which we feel to be ourselves.

It is sometimes thought that the emotions are the governing power in our nature. But I think all of us know, as a matter of practical experience, that there is something within us, behind our emotions and behind our wishes, an independent self, that, after all, decides everything and controls everything. Our emotions belong to us and are suffered and enjoyed by us, but they are not ourselves; and if God is to take possession of us, it must be into this central will or personality that He enters. If, then, He is reigning there by the power of His Spirit, all the rest of our nature must come under His sway; and as the will is, so is the man.

The practical bearing of this truth upon the difficulty I am considering is very great. For the decisions of our will are often so directly opposed to the decisions of our emotions that, if we are in the habit of considering our emotions as the test, we shall be very apt to feel like hypocrites in declaring those things to be real which our will alone had decided.

But the moment we see that the will is king, we shall utterly disregard anything that clamors against it, and shall claim as real its decisions, let the emotions rebel as they may.

I am aware that this is a difficult subject to deal with; but it is so exceedingly practical in its bearing upon the life of faith that I beg of you, dear reader, not to turn from it until you have mastered it.

Perhaps an illustration will help you. A young man of great intelligence, seeking to enter into this new life, was utterly discouraged at finding himself the slave to an inveterate habit of doubting. To his emotions nothing seemed true, nothing seemed real; and the more he struggled, the more unreal did it all become. He was told this secret concerning the will: that if he would only put his will over on the believing side, if he would choose to believe, if, in short, he would in this ego of his nature say, "I will believe! I do believe!" he need not then trouble about his emotions, for they would find themselves compelled, sooner or later, to come into harmony. "What!" he said. "Do you mean to tell me that I can *choose* to believe in that bold way, when nothing seems true to me? And will that kind of believing be real?" "Yes," was the answer. "It will. Fenelon says that true religion resides in the will alone; and he means that, since a man's will is really the man's self, of course, what his will does, he does. Your part then is simply to put your will, in this matter of believing, over on God's side, making up your mind that you will believe what He says because He says it, and that you will not pay any regard to the feelings that make it seem so unreal. God will not fail to respond, sooner or later, with His revelation to such a faith."

The young man paused a moment and then said solemnly, "I understand and will do what you say. I cannot control my emotions, but I can control my will; and the new life begins to look possible to me, if it is only my will that needs to be set straight in the matter. I can give my will to God, and I do."

From that moment, disregarding all the pitiful clamoring of his emotions, which continually accused him of being a wretched hypocrite, this young man held on steadily to the decision of his will, answering every accusation with the continued assertion that he chose to believe, he meant to believe, he did believe; until at the end of a few days he found himself triumphant, with every emotion and every thought brought into captivity to the power of the Spirit of God, who had taken possession of the will thus put into His hands. He had held fast the *profession* of his faith without wavering, although it had seemed to him that, as to real faith itself, he had none to hold fast. At times it had drained all the willpower he possessed to his lips, to say that he believed, so contrary was it to all the evidence of his senses or of his emotions. But he had caught the idea that his will was, after all, himself, and that if he kept that on God's side, he was doing all he could do, and that God alone could change his emotions or control his being. The result has been one of the grandest Christian lives I know of in its marvelous simplicity, directness, and power over sin.

The secret lies just here—that our will, which is the spring of all our actions, has been in the past under the control of sin and self, and these have worked in us all their own good pleasure. But now God calls upon us to yield our wills up unto Him, that He may take the control of them, and may work in us to will and to do of His good pleasure. If we will obey this call and present ourselves to Him as a living sacrifice, He will take possession of our surrendered wills and will begin at once to work in us "that which is well pleasing in his sight, through Jesus Christ," giving us the mind that was in Christ and transforming us into His image (see Romans 12:1–2).

Let us take another illustration. A lady who had entered into this life hid with Christ was confronted by a great prospective trial. Every emotion she had within her rose up in rebellion against it; and had she considered her emotions to be her king, she would have been in utter despair. But she had learned this secret of the will, and knowing that, at the bottom, she herself did really choose the will of God for her portion, she did not pay the slightest attention to her emotions but persisted in meeting every thought concerning the trial with the words, repeated over and over, "Thy will be done! Thy will be done!" asserting, in the face of all her rebelling feelings, that she did submit her will to God's, that she chose to submit it, and that His will should be and was her delight! The result was that in an incredibly short space of time every thought was brought into captivity, and she began to find even her very emotions rejoicing in the will of God.

Again, there was a lady who had a besetting sin, which in her emotions she dearly loved, but which in her will she hated. Believing herself to be necessarily under the control of her emotions, she had fully supposed she was unable to conquer it unless her emotions should first be changed. But she learned this secret concerning the will, and going to her closet she said, "Lord, Thou seest that with my emotions I love this sin, but in my real central self I hate it. Until now my emotions have had the mastery; but now I put my will into Thy hands and give it up to Thy working. I will never again consent in my will to yield to this sin. Take possession of my will and work in me to will and to do of Thy good pleasure."

Immediately she began to find deliverance. The Lord took possession of the will thus surrendered to Himself and began to work in her by His own power, so that His will in the matter gained the mastery over her emotions, and she found herself delivered, not by the power of an outward commandment, but by the inward power of the Spirit of God, "working in her that which was well pleasing in his sight."

And now, dear Christian, let me show you how to apply this principle to your difficulties. Cease to consider your emotions, for they are only the servants; and regard simply your will, which is the real king in your being. Is that given up to God? Is that put into His hands? Does your will decide to believe? Does your will choose to obey? If this is the case, then *you* are in the Lord's hands, and you decide to believe, and you choose to obey; for your will is yourself. And the thing is done. The transaction with God is as real, when only your will acts, as where every emotion coincides. It does not seem as real to you; but in God's sight it is as real. And when you have got hold of this secret and have discovered that you need not attend to your emotions but simply to the state of your will, all the scripture commands to yield yourself to God, to present yourself a living sacrifice to Him, to abide in Christ, to walk in the light, to die to self, become possible to you; for you are conscious that in all these your will can act and can take God's side; whereas, if it had been your emotions that must do it, you would, knowing them to be utterly uncontrollable, sink down in helpless despair.

When, then, this feeling of unreality or hypocrisy comes, do not be troubled by it. It is only in your emotions, and is not worth a moment's thought. Only see to it that your will is in God's hands, that your inward self is abandoned to His working, that your choice, your decision, is on His side; and there leave it. Your surging emotions, like a tossing vessel at anchor, which by degrees yields to the steady pull of the cable, finding themselves attached to the mighty power of God by the choice of your will, must inevitably come into captivity and give in their allegiance to Him; and you will sooner or later verify the truth of the saying that, "if any man will do his will, he shall know of the doctrine."

The will is like a wise mother in a nursery; the feelings are like a set of clamoring, crying children. The mother makes up her mind to a certain course of action which she believes to be right and best. The children clamor against it and declare it shall not be. But the mother, knowing that she is mistress and not they, pursues her course lovingly and calmly in spite of all their clamors; and the result is that the children are sooner or later won over to the mother's course of action and fall in with her decisions, and all is harmonious and happy. But if that mother should for a moment let in the thought that the children were the masters instead of herself, confusion would reign unchecked. And in how many souls at this very moment is there nothing but confusion, simply because the feelings are allowed to govern instead of the will?

Remember, then, that the real thing in your experience is what your will decides and not the verdict of your emotions; and that you are far more in danger of hypocrisy and untruth in yielding to the assertions of your feelings than in holding fast to the decision of your will. So that, if your will is on God's side, you are no hypocrite at this moment in claiming as your own the blessed reality of belonging altogether to Him even though your emotions may all declare the contrary.

I am convinced that throughout the Bible the expressions concerning the "heart" do not mean the emotions, that which we now understand by the word "heart," but they mean the will, the personality of the man, the man's own central self; and that the object of God's dealing with man is that this "I" may be yielded up to Him, and this central life abandoned to His entire control. It is not the feelings of the man God wants, but the man himself.

But do not let us make a mistake here. I say we must "give up" our wills, but I do not mean we are to be left will-less. We are not so to give up our wills as to be left like limp nerveless creatures, without any will at all. We are simply to substitute for our foolish, misdirected wills of ignorance and immaturity, the higher, divine, mature will of God. If we lay the emphasis on the word "our," we shall understand it better. The will we are to give up is our will, as it is misdirected and so parted off from God's will, not our will when it is one with God's will; for when our will is in harmony with His will, when it has the stamp of oneness with Him, it would be wrong for us to give it up.

The child is required to give up the misdirected will that belongs to it *as a child*, and we cannot let it say "I will" or "I will not"; but when its will is in harmony with ours, we want it to say "I will" or "I will not" with all the force of which it is capable.

When God is "working in us to will," we must set our faces like a flint to carry out this will and must respond with an emphatic "I will" to every "Thou shalt" of His. For God can only carry out His own will with us as we consent to it and will to be in harmony with Him.

Have you thus consented, dear reader, and is your face set as a flint to will what God wills? He wills that you should be entirely surrendered to Him, and that you should trust Him perfectly. Do you will the same?

Again I repeat, it is all in the will. Fenelon says, "The will to love God is the whole of religion." If, therefore, you have in your will taken the steps of surrender and faith, it is your right to believe even now, no matter how much your feelings may clamor against it, that you *are* all the Lord's, and that He *has* begun to "work in you both to will and to do of his good pleasure."

After this chapter was first written some years ago, the

following remarkable practical illustration of its teaching was handed to me by Pasteur Theodore Monod, of Paris. It is the experience of a Presbyterian minister, which this Pasteur had carefully kept for many years:

Newburgh, Sept. 26, 1842

Dear Brother—I take a few moments of that time which I have devoted to the Lord, in writing a short epistle to you, His servant. It is sweet to feel we are wholly the Lord's, that He has received us and called us His. This is religion, a relinquishment of the principle of self-ownership and the adoption in full of the abiding sentiment, "I am not my own, I am bought with a price." Since I last saw you I have been pressing forward, and yet there has been nothing remarkable in my experience of which I can speak; indeed, I do not know that it is best to look for remarkable things; but strive to be holy, as God is holy, pressing right on toward the mark of the prize.

I do not feel myself qualified to instruct you: I can only tell you the way in which I was led. The Lord deals differently with different souls, and we ought not to attempt to copy the experience of others; yet there are certain things which must be attended to by every one who is seeking after a clean heart.

There must be a personal consecration of all to God; a covenant made with God that we will be wholly and forever His. This I made intellectually, without any change in my feelings, with a heart full of hardness and darkness, unbelief and sin and insensibility.

I covenanted to be the Lord's and laid all upon the altar, a living sacrifice, to the best of my ability. And after I rose from my knees I was conscious of no change in my feelings. I was painfully conscious that there was no change. But yet I was sure that I did, with all the sincerity and honesty of purpose of which I was capable, make an entire and eternal consecration of myself to God. I did not then consider the work as done by any means, but I engaged to abide in a state of entire devotion to God, a living perpetual sacrifice. And now came the effort to do this.

I knew also that I must believe that God did accept me and did come to dwell in my heart. I was conscious I did not believe this, and yet I desired to do so. I read with much prayer John's first epistle and endeavored to assure my heart of God's love to me as an individual. I was sensible that my heart was full of evil. I seemed to have no power to overcome pride or to repel evil thoughts which I abhorred. But Christ was manifested to destroy the works of the devil, and it was clear that the sin in my heart was the work of the devil. I was enabled, therefore, to believe that God was working *in* me to will and to do, while I was working *out* my own salvation with fear and trembling.

I was convinced of unbelief, that it made the faithful God a liar. The Lord brought before me my besetting sins which had dominion over me, especially preaching myself instead of Christ and indulging in self-complacent thoughts after preaching. I was enabled to make myself of no reputation and to seek the honor which cometh from God only. Satan struggled hard to beat me back from the Rock of Ages; but thanks to God, I finally hit upon the method of living by the moment, and then I found rest.

I felt shut up to a momentary dependence upon the grace of Christ. I would not permit the adversary to trouble me about the past or future, for I each moment looked for the supply for that moment. I agreed that I would be a child of Abraham and walk by naked faith in the Word of God and not by inward feelings and emotions; I would seek to be a Bible Christian. *Since that time the Lord has given me a steady victory over sins which before enslaved me.* I delight in the Lord and in His word. I delight in my work as a minister; my fellowship is with the Father and with His Son Jesus Christ. I am a babe in Christ; I know my progress has been small compared with that made by many. My feelings vary; but when I have feelings I praise God and trust in His word; and when I am empty and my feelings are gone, I do the same. I have covenanted to walk by faith and not by feelings.

The Lord, I think, is beginning to revive His work among my people. "Praise the Lord!" May the Lord fill you with all His fullness and give you all the mind of Christ. Oh, be faithful! Walk before God and be perfect. Preach the Word. Be instant in season and out of season. The Lord loves you. He works with you. Rest your soul fully upon that promise, "Lo, I am with you alway, even unto the end of the world."

Your fellow-soldier,
William Hill

Chapter 8

Difficulties Concerning Guidance

You have now begun, dear reader, the life of faith. You have given yourself to the Lord to be His wholly and altogether, and you are now entirely in His hands to be molded and fashioned according to His own divine purpose into a vessel unto His honor. Your one most earnest desire is to follow Him whithersoever He may lead you and to be very pliable in His hands; and you are trusting Him to "work in you both to will and to do of his good pleasure." But you find a great difficulty here. You have not learned yet to know the voice of the good shepherd and are, therefore, in great doubt and perplexity as to what really is His will concerning you.

Perhaps there are certain paths into which God seems to be calling you, of which your friends disapprove. And these friends, it may be, are older than yourself in the Christian life and seem to you also to be much further advanced. You can scarcely bear to differ from them or to distress them; and you feel also very diffident of yielding to any seeming impressions of duty of which they do not approve. And yet you cannot get rid of these impressions, and you find yourself therefore plunged into great doubt and uneasiness.

There is a way out of all these difficulties to the fully

surrendered soul. I would repeat *fully* surrendered because, if there is any reserve of will upon any point, it becomes almost impossible to find out the mind of God in reference to that point; and therefore, the first thing is to be sure that you really do *purpose* to obey the Lord in every respect. If, however, this is your purpose, and your soul only needs to know the will of God in order to consent to it, then you surely cannot doubt His willingness to make His will known and to guide you in the right paths. There are many very clear promises in reference to this. Take, for instance, John 10:3–4, "He calleth his own sheep by name, and leadeth them out. And when he putteth forth his own sheep, he goeth before them, and the sheep follow him: for they know his voice." Or John 14:26: "But the Comforter, which is the Holy Ghost, whom the Father will send in my name, he shall teach you all things, and bring all things to your remembrance, whatsoever I have said unto you." Or James 1:5: "If any of you lack wisdom, let him ask of God, that giveth to all men liberally, and upbraideth not; and it shall be given him."

With such declarations as these and many more like them, we must believe that divine guidance is promised to us, and our faith must therefore confidently look for and expect it. This is essential, for in James 1:6–7, we are told, "Let him ask in faith, nothing wavering. For he that wavereth is like a wave of the sea driven with the wind and tossed. For let not that man think that he shall receive any thing of the Lord."

Settle this point then, first of all, and let no suggestion of doubt turn you from a steadfast faith in regard to it, that divine guidance has been promised, and that, if you seek it, you are sure to receive it.

Next, you must remember that our God has all knowledge and all wisdom, and that, therefore, it is very possible

He may guide you into paths wherein *He* knows great blessings are awaiting you, but which, to the short-sighted human eyes around you, seem sure to result in confusion and loss. You must recognize the fact that God's thoughts are not as man's thoughts, nor His ways as man's ways; and that He alone, who knows the end of things from the beginning, can judge of what the results of any course of action may be. You must, therefore, realize that His very love for you may perhaps lead you to run counter to the loving wishes of even your dearest friends. You must learn from Luke 14:26–33 and similar passages, that in order to be a disciple and follower of your Lord, you may perhaps be called upon to forsake inwardly all that you have, even father or mother, or brother or sister, or husband or wife, or it may be your own life also. Unless the possibility of this is clearly recognized, you will be very likely to get into difficulty because it often happens that the child of God who enters upon this life of obedience is sooner or later led into paths which meet with the disapproval of those he best loves; and unless he is prepared for this and can trust the Lord through it all, he will scarcely know what to do.

But, these points having all been settled, we come now to the question as to how God's guidance is to come to us and how we shall be able to know His voice. There are four ways in which He reveals His will to us—through the scriptures, through providential circumstances, through the convictions of our own higher judgment, and through the inward impressions of the Holy Spirit on our minds. Where these four harmonize, it is safe to say that God speaks. For I lay it down as a foundation principle, which no one can gainsay, that of course His voice will always be in harmony with itself, no matter in how many different ways He may speak. The voices may be many; the message can be but one. If God tells me in one voice to do or to leave undone anything, He cannot possibly tell me the opposite in another voice. If there is a contradiction in the voices, the speakers cannot be the same. Therefore, my rule for distinguishing the voice of God would be to bring it to the test of this harmony.

The scriptures come first. If you are in doubt upon any subject, you must, first of all, consult the Bible about it and see whether there is any law there to direct you. Until you have found and obeyed God's will as it is there revealed, you must not ask nor expect a separate, direct, personal revelation. A great many fatal mistakes are made in the matter of guidance by the overlooking of this simple rule. Where our Father has written out for us a plain direction about anything, He will not, of course, make a special revelation to us about that thing. And if we fail to search out and obey the scripture rule, where there is one, and look instead for an inward voice, we shall open ourselves to delusions and shall almost inevitably get into error. No man, for instance, needs or could expect any direct personal revelation to tell him not to steal because God has already in the scriptures plainly declared His will about stealing. This seems such an obvious thing that I would not speak of it, but I have frequently met with Christians who have altogether overlooked it, and who have, as the result, gone off into fanaticism. I knew one earnest Christian who had the text "All things are yours" so strongly impressed upon her mind in reference to some money belonging to a friend, that she felt it was a direct command to her to steal that money; and after a great struggle she obeyed this apparent guidance, with, of course, most grievous after results. Had she submitted her "leading" to the plain teaching of scripture in reference to stealing, she would have been saved.

The Bible, it is true, does not always give a rule for every particular course of action, and in these cases we need and must expect guidance in other ways. But the scriptures are far more explicit, even about details, than most people think, and there are not many important affairs in life for which a clear direction may not be found in God's book. Take the matter of dress, and we have 1 Peter 3:3–4 and 1 Timothy 2:9. Take the matter of conversation, and we have Ephesians 4:29 and 5:4. Take the matter of avenging injuries and standing up for our rights, and we have Romans 12:19–21 and Matthew 5:38–48 and 1 Peter 2:19–21. Take the matter of forgiving one another, and we have Ephesians 4:32 and Mark 11:25–26. Take the matter of conformity to the world, and we have Romans 12:2 and 1 John 2:15–17 and James 4:4. Take the matter of anxieties of every kind, and we have Matthew 6:25–34 and Philippians 4:6–7.

I only give these as examples to show how very full and practical the Bible's guidance is. If, therefore, you find yourself in perplexity, first of all search and see whether the Bible speaks on the point in question, asking God to make plain to you, by the power of His Spirit, through the scriptures, what is His mind. And whatever shall seem to you to be plainly taught there, that you must obey. No special guidance will ever be given about a point on which the scriptures are explicit, nor could any guidance ever be contrary to the scriptures.

It is essential, however, in this connection to remember that the Bible is a book of principles and not a book of disjointed aphorisms. Isolated texts may often be made to sanction things to which the principles of scripture are totally opposed. I believe all fanaticism comes in this way. An isolated text is so impressed upon the mind that it seems a necessity to obey it, no matter into what wrong thing it may lead; and thus the principles of scripture are violated, under the very plea of obedience to the scriptures. In Luke 4 the enemy is represented as using isolated texts to endorse his temptations, while Christ repelled him by announcing principles.

If, however, upon searching the Bible you do not find any principles that will settle your special point of difficulty, you must then seek guidance in the other ways mentioned; and God will surely voice Himself to you, either by a conviction of your judgment, or by providential circumstances, or by a clear inward impression. In all true guidance these four voices will, as I have said, necessarily harmonize, for God cannot say in one voice that which He contradicts in another. Therefore, if you have an impression of duty, you must see whether it is in accordance with scripture, and whether it commends itself to your own higher judgment, and also whether, as we Quakers say, the "way opens" for its carrying out. If any one of these tests fails, it is not safe to proceed, but you must wait in quiet trust until the Lord shows you the point of harmony, which He surely will, sooner or later, if it is His voice that is speaking. Anything which is out of this divine harmony must be rejected, therefore, as not coming from God. For we must never forget that "impressions" can come from other sources as well as from the Holy Spirit. The strong personalities of those around us are the source of a great many of our impressions. Impressions also arise often from our wrong physical conditions, which color things far more than we dream. And finally, impressions come from those spiritual enemies which seem to lie in wait for every traveler who seeks to enter the higher regions of the spiritual life. In the same epistle which tells us that we are seated in "heavenly places in Christ" (Ephesians 2:6), we are also told that we shall have to fight there with spiritual enemies (Ephesians 6:12). These spiritual enemies, whoever or whatever they may be, must necessarily communicate with us by means of our spiritual faculties; and their voices, therefore, will be, as the voice of God is, an inward impression made upon our spirits. Consequently, just as the Holy Spirit may tell us by impressions what is the will of God concerning us, so also will these spiritual enemies tell us by impressions what is their will concerning us, disguising themselves, of course, as "angels of light" who have come to lead us closer to God.

Many earnest and honest-hearted children of God have been thus deluded into paths of extreme fanaticism, while all the while thinking they were closely following the Lord. God, who sees the sincerity of their hearts, can and does, I am sure, pity and forgive; but the consequences as to this life are often very sad. It is not enough to have a "leading"; we must find out the source of that leading before we give ourselves up to follow it. It is not enough, either, for the leading to be very "remarkable," or the coincidences to be very striking, to stamp it as being surely from God. In all ages of the world evil and deceiving agencies have been able to work miracles, foretell events, reveal secrets, and give "signs"; and God's people have always been emphatically warned about being deceived thereby.

It is essential, therefore, that our "leadings" should all be tested by the teachings of scripture. But this alone is not enough. They must be tested as well by our own spiritually enlightened judgment or what is familiarly called "common sense."

So far as I can see, the scriptures everywhere make it an essential thing for the children of God, in their journey through this world, to use all the faculties that have been given them. They are to use their outward faculties for their outward walk and their inward faculties for their inward walk; and they might as well expect to be "kept" from dashing their feet against a stone in the outward if they walk blindfold, as to be "kept" from spiritual stumbling if they put aside their judgment and common sense in their interior life.

Some, however, may say here, "But I thought we were not to depend on our human understanding in divine things." I answer to this that we are not to depend on our unenlightened human understanding, but upon our human judgment and common sense enlightened by the Spirit of God. That is, God will speak to us through the faculties He has Himself given us and not independently of them; so that just as we are to use our outward eyes in our outward walk, no matter how full of faith we may be, so also we are to use the interior "eyes of our understanding" in our interior walk with God.

The third test to which our impressions must be brought is that of providential circumstances. If a "leading" is of God, the way will always open for it. Our Lord assures us of this when He says, in John 10:4, "And when he putteth forth his own sheep, *he goeth before them*, and the sheep *follow* him: for they know his voice." Notice here the expressions "goeth before" and "follow." He goes before to open a way, and we are to follow in the way thus opened. It is never a sign of a divine leading when the Christian insists on opening his own way and riding roughshod over all opposing things. If the Lord "goes before" us, He will open the door for us, and we shall not need to batter down doors for ourselves.

The fourth point I would make is this—that, just as our impressions must be tested, as I have shown, by the other three voices, so must these other voices be tested by our inward impressions; and if we feel a "stop in our minds" about anything, we must wait until that is removed before acting. A Christian who had advanced with unusual rapidity in the divine life gave me, as her secret, this simple receipt: "I always mind the checks." We must not ignore the voice of our inward impressions, nor ride roughshod over them, any more than we must the other three voices of which I have spoken.

Every peculiarly precious spiritual gift is always necessarily linked with some peculiar danger. When the spiritual world is opened to a soul, both the good and the evil there will meet it. But we must not be discouraged by this. Who would not rather take manhood with all its risks and dangers than remain forever in the ignorance and innocence of childhood; and who would not rather grow up into the stature of Christ, even if it shall involve new and more subtle forms of temptation?

Therefore, we must not be deterred from embracing the blessed privilege of divine guidance by a dread of the dangers that environ it. With the four tests I have mentioned and a divine sense of "oughtness" derived from the harmony of all of God's voices, there need be nothing to fear. And to me it seems that the blessedness and joy of this direct communication of God's will to us is one of our grandest privileges. That God *cares* enough about us to desire to regulate the details of our lives is the strongest proof of love He could give; and that He should condescend to tell us all about it and to let us know just how to live and walk so as perfectly to please Him seems almost too good to be true. We never care about the little details of people's lives unless we love them. It is a matter of indifference to us what the majority of people we meet do or how they spend their time. But as soon as we begin to love anyone, we begin at once to care. God's law, therefore, is only another name of God's love; and the more minutely that law descends into the details of our lives, the more sure we are made of the depth and reality of the love. We can never know the full joy and privileges of the life hid with Christ in God until we have learned the lesson of daily and hourly guidance.

God's promise is that He will work in us to *will* as well as to do of His good pleasure. This means, of course, that He will take possession of our will and work it for us; and that His suggestions will come to us, not so much as commands from the outside as desires springing up within. They will originate in our will; we shall feel as though we *desired* to do so and so, not as though we *must*. And this makes it a service of perfect liberty; for it is always easy to do what we desire to do, let the accompanying circumstances be as difficult as they may. Every mother knows that she could secure perfect and easy obedience in her child if she could only get into that child's will and work it for him, making him want himself to do the things she willed he should. And this is what our Father, in the new dispensation, does for His children; He "writes his laws on our hearts and on our minds," so that our affection and our understanding embrace them, and we are *drawn* to obey instead of being *driven* to it.

The way in which the Holy Spirit, therefore, usually works in a fully obedient soul in regard to this direct guidance is to impress upon the mind a wish or desire to do or to leave undone certain things.

The child of God when engaged in prayer feels, perhaps, a sudden suggestion made to his inmost consciousness in reference to a certain point of duty. "I would like to do this or the other," he thinks; "I wish I could." At once this matter should be committed to the Lord, with an instant consent of the will to obey Him, should the suggestion prove to be really from Him. And then the tests I have mentioned should be intelligently applied, namely, as to whether the suggestion is in accordance with the teaching of scripture, with a sanctified judgment, and with providential circumstances. Often no distinct consciousness of this process is necessary as our spiritual intelligence can see at a glance the right or wrong of the matter. But, however it may come, when the divine harmony is reached and the divine sense of "oughtness" settles down on the heart, then an immediate obedience is the safest and easiest course. The first moment that we clearly see a thing to be right is always the moment when it is easy to do it. If we "let in the reasoner," as the Quakers express it, the golden opportunity is lost, and obedience becomes more and more difficult with every moment's delay. The old self-will wakens into life; and the energies that should have been occupied with obeying are absorbed instead in the struggle with doubts and reasonings.

It sometimes happens, however, that, in spite of all our efforts to discover the truth, the divine sense of "oughtness" does not seem to come, and our doubts and perplexities continue unenlightened. In addition to this, our friends differ from us and would, we know, oppose our course. In such a case there is nothing to do but to wait until the light comes. But we must wait in faith, and in an attitude of entire surrender, saying a continual "Yes" to the will of our Lord, let it be what it may. If the suggestion is from Him, it will continue and strengthen; if it is not from Him, it will disappear, and we shall almost forget we ever had it. If it continues, if every time we are brought into near communion with the Lord it seems to return, if it troubles us in our moments of prayer and disturbs all our peace, and if finally it conforms to the test of the divine harmony of which I have spoken, we may then feel sure it is from God, and we must yield to it or suffer an unspeakable loss.

The apostle gives us a rule in reference to doubtful things, which seems to me very explicit. He is speaking about certain kinds of meat eating which were ceremoniously unclean, and after declaring his own liberty says, "I know, and am persuaded by the Lord Jesus, that there is nothing unclean of itself: but to him that esteemeth any thing to be unclean, to him it is unclean." And in summing up the whole subject he writes: "Hast thou faith? have it to thyself before God. Happy is he that condemneth not himself in that thing which he alloweth. And he that doubteth is damned [condemned] if he eat, because he eateth not of faith: for whatsoever is not of faith is sin." In all doubtful things you must stand still and refrain from action until God gives you light to know more clearly His mind concerning them. Very often you will find that the doubt has been His voice calling upon you to come into more perfect conformity to His will; but sometimes these doubtful things are only temptations, or morbid feelings, to which it would be most unwise for you to yield, and the only safe way is to wait until you can act in faith, for "whatsoever is not of faith is sin."

Take all your present perplexities, then, to the Lord. Tell Him you only want to know and obey His voice, and ask Him to make it plain to you. Promise Him that you will obey, whatever it may be. Believe implicitly that He is guiding you according to His Word. In all doubtful things, wait for clear light. Look and listen for His voice continually; and the moment you are sure of it, then, but not until then, yield an immediate obedience. Trust Him to make you forget the impression if it is not His will; and if it continues and is in harmony with all His other voices, do not be afraid to obey.

Above everything else, trust Him. Nowhere is faith more needed than here. He has promised to guide. You have asked Him to do it. And now you must believe that He does, and must take what comes as being His guidance. No earthly parent or master could guide his children or servants, if they should refuse to take his commands as being really the expression of his will; and God *cannot* guide those souls who never trust Him enough to believe that He is doing it.

Above all, do not be afraid of this blessed life, lived hour by hour and day by day under the guidance of your Lord! If He seeks to bring you out of the world and into very close conformity to Himself, do not shrink from it. It is your most blessed privilege. Rejoice in it. Embrace it eagerly. Let everything go that it may be yours.

God only is the creature's home,
*   Though rough and strait the road;*
Yet nothing else can satisfy
*   The love that longs for God.*

How little of that road, my soul!
*   How little hast thou gone!*
Take heart and let the thought of God
*   Allure thee farther on.*

Dole not thy duties out to God,
*   But let thy hand be free;*
Look long at Jesus—His sweet love
*   How was it dealt to thee?*

The perfect way is hard to flesh,
*   It is not hard to love;*
If thou wert sick for want of God,
*   How swiftly wouldst thou move!*

And only this perfection needs
*   A heart kept calm all day,*
To catch the words the Spirit there
*   From hour to hour may say.*

Then keep thy conscience sensitive,
*   No inward token miss;*
And go where grace entices thee—
*   Perfection lies in this.*

Be docile to thine unseen guide,
*   Love Him as He loves thee;*
Time and obedience are enough,
*   And thou a saint shall be.*

Chapter 9

Difficulties Concerning Doubts

A great many Christians are slaves to an inveterate habit of doubting. I do not mean doubts as to the existence of God or the truths of the Bible, but doubts as to their own personal relations with the God in whom they profess to believe, doubts as to the forgiveness of their sins, doubts as to their hopes of heaven, and doubts about their own inward experience. No drunkards are ever more in bondage to their habit of drink than they are to their habit of doubting. Every step of their spiritual progress is taken against the fearful odds of an army of doubts that are forever lying in wait to assail them at each favorable moment. Their lives are made wretched, their usefulness is effectually hindered, and their communion with God is continually broken by their doubts. And although the entrance of the soul upon the life of faith does, in many cases, take it altogether out of the region where these doubts live and flourish, yet even here it sometimes happens that the old tyrant will rise up and reassert his sway and will cause the feet to stumble and the heart to fail, even when he cannot succeed in utterly turning the believer back into the dreary wilderness again.

All of us remember, doubtless, our childish fascination, and yet horror, in the story of Christian's imprisonment in

Doubting Castle by the wicked giant Despair, and our exultant sympathy in his escape through those massive gates and from the cruel tyrant. Little did we suspect then that we should ever find ourselves taken prisoner by the same giant and imprisoned in the same castle. But I fear that each one of us, if we were perfectly honest, would have to confess to at least one such experience and some of us perhaps to a great many.

It seems strange that people, whose very name of believers implies that their one chiefest characteristic is that they believe, should have to confess that they have doubts. And yet it is such a universal habit, and I feel, if the name were to be given over again, the only fitting and descriptive name that could be given to many of God's children would have to be that of doubters. In fact, most Christians have settled down under their doubts, as to a sort of inevitable malady from which they suffer acutely but to which they must try to be resigned as a part of the necessary discipline of this earthly life; and they lament over their doubts as a man might lament over his rheumatism, making themselves out as "interesting cases" of special and peculiar trial, which require the tenderest sympathy and the utmost consideration.

This is too often true even of believers who are earnestly longing to enter upon the life and walk of faith and who have made, perhaps, many steps toward it. They have gotten rid, it may be, of the old doubts that once tormented them, as to whether their sins are really forgiven and whether they shall, after all, get safe to heaven; but they have not gotten rid of doubting. They have simply shifted the habit to a higher platform. They are saying, perhaps, "Yes, I believe my sins are forgiven, and I am a child of God through faith in Jesus Christ. I dare not doubt this any more. But then—" and this "but then" includes an interminable array of doubts concerning most of the declarations and promises our

Father has made to His children. One after another they fight with these promises and refuse to believe them until they can have some more reliable proof of their being true than the simple word of their God; and then they wonder why they are permitted to walk in such darkness and look upon themselves almost in the light of martyrs and groan under the peculiar spiritual conflicts they are compelled to endure.

Spiritual conflicts! Far better would they be named did we call them spiritual rebellions! Our fight is to be a fight of faith; and the moment we let in doubts, our fight ceases, and our rebellion begins.

I desire to put forth, if possible, a vigorous protest against this whole thing.

Just as well might I join in with the laments of a drunkard and unite with him in prayer for grace to endure the discipline of his fatal appetite as to give way for one instant to the weak complaints of these enslaved souls and try to console them under their slavery. To one and to the other I would dare to do nothing else but proclaim the perfect deliverance which the Lord Jesus Christ has in store for them and beseech, entreat, and importune them, with all the power at my command, to avail themselves of it and be free. Not for one moment would I listen to their despairing excuses. You ought to be free; you can be free; you must be free!

Will you undertake to tell me that it is an inevitable necessity for God to be doubted by His children? Is it an inevitable necessity for your children to doubt you? Would you tolerate their doubts a single hour? Would you pity your son and condole with him and feel that he was an "interesting case" if he should come to you and say, "Father, I am such a doubter that I cannot believe I am your child or that you really love me"? And yet how often we hear a child of God excuse himself for his doubts by saying, "Oh, but I am such a doubter that I cannot believe in God's love and forgiveness"; and no one seems shocked at it. You might just as well say, with a like complacency, "Oh, but I am such a liar that I cannot help telling lies," and expect people to consider it a sufficient excuse. In the sight of God, I verily believe doubting is in some cases as displeasing as lying. It certainly is more dishonoring to Him, for it impugns His truthfulness and defames His character. John says that "he that believeth not God hath made him a liar," and it seems to me that hardly anything could be worse than thus to fasten on God the character of being a liar! Have you ever thought of this as the result of your doubting?

I remember seeing once the indignation and sorrow of a mother's heart deeply stirred by a little doubting on the part of one of her children. She had brought two little girls to my house, to leave them while she did some errands. One of them, with the happy confidence of childhood, abandoned herself to all the pleasures she could find in my nursery and sang and played until her mother's return. The other one, with the wretched caution and mistrust of maturity, sat down alone in a corner to wonder, first, whether her mother would remember to come back for her and to fear she would be forgotten and then to imagine her mother would be glad of the chance to get rid of her anyhow because she was such a naughty girl; and ended with working herself up into a perfect frenzy of despair. The look on that mother's face, when upon her return the weeping little girl told what was the matter with her, I shall not easily forget. Grief, wounded love, indignation, and pity all strove together for mastery: and the mother hardly knew who was most at fault, herself or the child, that such doubts should be possible.

Perhaps such doubts might be possible with an earthly mother, but never, never with God; and a hundred times in my life since, has that scene come up before me with deepest teaching and has compelled me, peremptorily, to refuse admittance to the doubts about my heavenly Father's love and care and remembrance of me that have clamored at the door of my heart for entrance.

Doubting is, I am convinced, to many people a real luxury, and to deny themselves this luxury would be the hardest piece of self-denial they have ever known. It is a luxury which, like the indulgence in some other luxuries, brings very sorrowful results; and perhaps, looking at the sadness and misery it has brought into your own Christian experience, you may be inclined to say, "Alas! It is no luxury to me, but only a fearful trial." But pause for a moment. Try giving it up, and you will soon find out whether it is a luxury or not. Do not your doubts come trooping to your door like a company of sympathizing friends who appreciate your hard case and have come to condole with you? And is it no luxury to sit down with them and entertain them, to listen to their arguments and join in with their condolences? Would it be no self-denial to turn resolutely from them and refuse to hear a word they have to say? If you do not know, try it and see.

Have you never tasted the luxury of indulging in hard thoughts against those who have, as you think, injured you? Have you never known what a positive fascination it is to brood over their unkindnesses and to pry into their malice and to imagine all sorts of wrong and uncomfortable things about them? It has made you wretched, of course; but it has been a fascinating sort of wretchedness that you could not easily give up.

Just like this is the luxury of doubting. Things have gone wrong with you in your experience. Dispensations have been mysterious; temptations have been peculiar; your "case" has seemed different from others. What is more natural than to conclude that for some reason God has forsaken you and does not love you and is indifferent to your welfare? How irresistible is the conviction that you are too wicked for Him to care for or too difficult for Him to manage!

You do not mean to blame Him or accuse Him of injustice, for you feel that His indifference and rejection of you are, because of your unworthiness, fully deserved; and this very subterfuge leaves you at liberty, under the guise of a just and true appreciation of your own shortcomings, to indulge in your dishonoring doubts. Although you think it is yourself you are doubting, you are really doubting the Lord and are indulging in as hard and wrong thoughts of Him as ever you did of a human enemy. For He declares that He came to save, not the righteous, but sinners; and your very sinfulness and unworthiness, instead of being a reason why He should not love you and care for you are really your chiefest claim upon His love and His care.

As well might the poor little lamb that has wandered from the flock and gotten lost in the wilderness say, "I am lost and, therefore, the shepherd cannot love me, nor care for me nor remember me; he only loves and cares for the lambs that never wander." As well might the ill man say, "I am ill and, therefore, the doctor will not come to see me nor give me any medicine; he only cares for and visits well people." Jesus says, "They that be whole need not a physician; but they that are sick." And again He says, "What man of you, having an hundred sheep, if he lose one of them, doth not leave the ninety and nine in the wilderness, and go after that which is lost, until he find it?" Any thoughts of Him, therefore, that are different from this which He Himself has said, are hard thoughts; and to indulge in them is far worse than to indulge in hard thoughts of any earthly friend or foe. From beginning to end of your Christian life, it is always sinful to indulge in doubts. Doubts and discouragements are all from an evil source and are always untrue. A direct and emphatic denial is the only way to meet them.

This brings me to the practical part of the whole subject, as to how to get deliverance from this fatal habit. My answer would be that the deliverance from this must be by the same means as the deliverance from any other sin. It is to be found in Christ, and in Him only. You must hand your doubting over to Him, as you have learned to hand your other temptations. You must do with it just what you do with your temper or your pride; that is, you must give it up to the Lord. I believe myself the only effectual remedy is to take a pledge against it, as you would urge a drunkard to do against drink, trusting in the Lord alone to keep you steadfast.

Like any other sin, the stronghold is in the will, and the will or purpose to doubt must be surrendered exactly as you surrender the will or purpose to yield to any other temptation. God always takes possession of a surrendered will; and if we come to the point of saying that we will not doubt and surrender this central fortress of our nature to Him, His blessed Spirit will begin at once to "work in us all the good pleasure of His will," and we shall find ourselves kept from doubting by His mighty and overcoming power.

The trouble is, that in this matter of doubting the Christian does not always make a full surrender but is apt to reserve a little secret liberty to doubt, looking upon it as being sometimes a necessity.

"I do not want to doubt any more," we will say, or, "I hope I shall not"; but it is hard to come to the point of saying, "I *will* not doubt again," and no surrender is effectual until it reaches the point of saying, "I will not." The liberty to doubt must be given up forever; and we must consent to a continuous life of inevitable trust. It is often necessary, I think, to make a definite transaction of this surrender of doubting and come to a point about it. I believe it is quite as necessary in the case of a doubter as in the case of a drunkard. It will not do to give it up by degrees. The total-abstinence principle is the only effectual one here.

Then, the surrender once made, we must rest absolutely upon the Lord for deliverance in each time of temptation. The moment the assault comes, we must lift up the shield of faith against it. We must hand the very first suggestion of doubt over to the Lord and must let Him manage it. We must refuse to entertain the doubt a single moment. Let it come ever so plausibly or under whatever guise of humility, we must simply say, "I dare not doubt; I must trust. God *is* my Father, and He does love me. Jesus saves me; He saves me now." Those three little words, repeated over and over, "Jesus saves me, Jesus saves me," will put to flight the greatest army of doubts that ever assaulted any soul. I have tried it times without number and have never known it to fail. Do not stop to argue out the matter with yourself or with your doubts. Pay no attention to them whatever, but treat them with the utmost contempt. Shut your door in their very face and emphatically deny every word they say to you. Bring up some "It is written" and hurl it after them. Look right at Jesus, and tell Him that you do trust Him and that you intend to go on trusting Him. Then let the doubts clamor as they may, they cannot hurt you if you will not let them in.

I know it will look to you sometimes as though you were shutting your door against your best friends, and your heart will long after your doubts more than ever the Israelites longed after the fleshpots of Egypt. But deny yourself; take up your cross in this matter, and quietly but firmly refuse ever to listen to a single word.

Often has it happened to me to find, on awaking in the morning, a perfect army of doubts clamoring at my door for admittance. Nothing has seemed real; nothing has seemed true; and least of all has it seemed possible that I—miserable, wretched I—could be the object of the Lord's love or care or notice. If I only had been at liberty to let these doubts in and invite them to take seats and make themselves at home, what a luxury I should many times have felt it to be! But years ago I made a pledge against doubting, and I would as soon think of violating my pledge against intoxicating liquor as of violating this one. I have never dared to admit the first doubt. At such times, therefore, I have been compelled to lift up the "shield of faith" the moment I have become conscious of these suggestions of doubt; and handing the whole army over to the Lord to conquer, I have begun to assert, over and over, my faith in Him, in the simple words, "God *is* my Father; I *am* His forgiven child; He *does* love me; Jesus saves me; Jesus saves me now!" The victory has always been complete. The enemy has come in like a flood, but the "Spirit of the Lord has lifted up a standard against him," and my doubts have been put to flight. And I have been able to join in the song of Moses and the children of Israel, saying, "I will sing unto the LORD, for he hath triumphed gloriously: the horse and rider hath he thrown into the sea. The LORD is my strength and song, and he is become my salvation."

Dear doubting souls, go and do likewise, and a similar victory shall be yours. You may think, perhaps, that doubts are a necessity in your case, owing to the peculiarity of your temperament; but I assure you most emphatically that this is not so. You are no more under a necessity to be doubtful as to your relationships to your heavenly Father than you are to be doubtful as to your relationships to your earthly father. In both cases the thing you must depend on is their word, not your feelings; and no earthly father has ever declared or manifested his fatherhood one thousandth part as unmistakably or as lovingly as your heavenly Father has declared and manifested His. If you would not "make God a liar," therefore, you must make your believing as inevitable and necessary a thing as your obedience. You would obey God, I believe, even though you should die in the act. Believe Him, also, even though the effort to believe should cost you your life. The conflict may be very severe; it may seem at times unendurable. But let your unchanging declaration be from henceforth, "Though he slay me, yet will I trust in him." When doubts come, meet them, not with arguments, but with assertions of faith. All doubts are an attack of the enemy; the Holy Spirit never suggests them, never. He is the comforter, not the accuser; and He never shows us our need without at the same time revealing the divine supply.

Do not give heed to your doubts, therefore, for a moment. Turn from them with horror, as you would from blasphemy; for they *are* blasphemy. You cannot, perhaps, hinder the suggestions of doubt from coming to you, any more than you can hinder the boys in the street from swearing as you go by; and consequently you are not sinning in the one case any more than in the other. But just as you can refuse to listen to the boys or join in their oaths, so can you also refuse to listen to the doubts or join in with them. They are not *your* doubts until you consent to them and adopt them as true. When they come, you must at once turn from them as you would from swearing. Often a very good practical way of getting rid of them is to go at once and confess your faith, in the strongest language possible, somewhere or to someone. If you cannot do this by word of mouth, write it in a letter, or repeat it over and over in your heart to the Lord.

As you lay down this book, therefore, take up your pen and write out your determination never to doubt again. Make it a real transaction between your soul and the Lord. Give up your liberty to doubt forever. Put your will in this matter over on the Lord's side, and trust Him to keep you from falling. Tell Him all about your utter weakness and your long-encouraged habits of doubt, and how helpless you are before it, and commit the whole battle to Him. Tell Him you *will* not doubt again, putting forth all your will-power on His side, and against His enemy and yours; and then, henceforward, keep your face steadfastly "looking unto Jesus," away from yourself and away from your doubts, holding fast the profession of your faith without wavering, because "He is faithful that hath promised." Rely on *His* faithfulness, not on your own. You have committed the keeping of your soul to Him as unto a "faithful Creator," and you must never again admit the possibility of His being unfaithful. Believe He is faithful, not because you feel it or see it, but because He says He is. Believe it, whether you feel it or not. Believe it, even when it seems to you that you are believing something that is absolutely untrue. Believe it actively, and believe it persistently. Cultivate a continuous habit of believing, and never let your faith waver for any "seeming," however plausible it may be. The result will be that sooner or later you will come to *know* that it is true, and all doubts will vanish in the blaze of the glory of the absolute faithfulness of God!

It is an inexorable rule in the spiritual life that according to our faith it is to be unto us; and of course this rule must work both ways and, therefore, we may fairly expect that it will be also unto us according to our doubts.

Doubts and discouragements are, I believe, inlets by which evil enters, while faith is an impregnable wall against all evil.

Dear doubting souls, my heart yearns over you with a tender sympathy! I know your sincerity and your earnestness, and your struggles after an abiding experience of peace with God, through the Lord Jesus Christ: and I know also how effectually your fatal habit of doubting has held you back. I would that my words might open your eyes to see the deliverance that lies at your very door. Try my plan, I beseech you, and see if it will not be true, that "according to your faith" it shall inevitably be unto you.

Chapter 10

Difficulties Concerning Temptations

Certain great mistakes are made concerning this matter of temptation in the practical working out of the life of faith.

First of all, people seem to expect, that, after the soul has entered into rest in the Lord, temptations will cease; and they think that the promised deliverance is to be not only from yielding to temptation but even also from being tempted. Consequently, when they find the "Canaanite still in the land," and see the "cities great and walled up to heaven," they are utterly discouraged and think they must have gone wrong in some way, and that this cannot be the true land, after all.

Then, next, they make the mistake of looking upon temptation as sin and of blaming themselves for suggestions of evil, even while they abhor them. This brings them into condemnation and discouragement; and discouragement, if continued in, always ends at last in actual sin. Sin makes an easy prey of a discouraged soul; so that we fall often from the very fear of having fallen.

To meet the first of these difficulties, it is only necessary to refer to the scripture declarations which state that the Christian life is to be throughout a warfare; and that it is to be especially so when we are "seated in heavenly places in Christ Jesus," and are called to wrestle against spiritual enemies, whose power and skill to tempt us must doubtless be far superior to any we have ever heretofore encountered. As a fact, temptations generally increase in strength tenfold after we have entered into the interior life, rather than decrease; and no amount or sort of them must ever for a moment lead us to suppose we have not really found the true abiding place. Strong temptations are often more a sign of great grace than of little grace.

When the children of Israel had first left Egypt, the Lord did not lead them through the country of the Philistines, although that was the nearest way; "for God said, Lest peradventure the people repent when they see war, and they return to Egypt." But afterwards, when they had learned how to trust Him better, he permitted their enemies to attack them. Moreover, even in their wilderness journey they met with but few enemies and fought but few battles compared to those they encountered in the land of Canaan, where they found seven great nations and thirty-one kings to be conquered, besides walled cities to be taken and giants to be overcome.

They could not have fought with the "Canaanites, and the Hittites, and the Amorites, and the Perizzites, and the Hivites, and the Jebusites," until they had gone in to the land where these enemies were. The very power of your temptations, dear Christian, therefore, may perhaps be one of the strongest proofs that you really are in the land of promise you have been seeking to enter because they are temptations peculiar to that land; consequently you must never allow them to cause you to question the fact of your having entered it.

The second mistake is not quite so easy to deal with. It seems hardly worthwhile to say that temptation is not sin, and yet much distress arises from not understanding this fact. The very suggestion of wrong seems to bring pollution with it; and the poor tempted soul begins to feel as if it must be very bad indeed and very far off from God to have had such thoughts and suggestions. It is as though a burglar should break into a man's house to steal and, when the master of the house begins to resist him and drive him out, should turn round and accuse the owner of being himself the thief. It is the enemy's grand ruse for entrapping us. He comes and whispers suggestions of evil to us—doubts, blasphemies, jealousies, envyings, and pride—and then turns round and says, "Oh, how wicked you must be to think such things! It is very plain that you are not trusting the Lord; for if you had been, it would be impossible for these things to have entered your heart."

This reasoning sounds so very plausible that we often accept it as true and so come under condemnation and are filled with discouragement; and then it is easy for temptation to develop into actual sin. One of the most fatal things in the life of faith is discouragement; one of the most helpful is confidence. A very wise man once said that in overcoming temptations confidence was the first thing, confidence the second, and confidence the third. We must *expect* to conquer. That is why the Lord said so often to Joshua, "Be strong and of good courage"; "Be not afraid, neither be thou dismayed"; "Only be thou strong and very courageous." And it is also the reason He says to us, "Let not your heart be troubled, neither let it be afraid." The power of temptation is in the fainting of our own hearts. The enemy knows this well, and he always begins his assaults by discouraging us, if he can in any way accomplish it.

This discouragement arises sometimes from what we think is a righteous grief and disgust at ourselves that such things *could* be any temptation to us but which is really mortification coming from the fact that we have been indulging in a secret self-congratulation that our tastes were too pure or our separation from the world was too complete for such things to tempt us. We are discouraged because we have expected something from ourselves and have been sorely disappointed not to find that something there. This mortification and discouragement, though they present an appearance of true humility, are really a far worse condition than the temptation itself, for they are nothing but the results of wounded self-love. True humility can bear to see its own utter weakness and foolishness revealed because it never expected anything from itself and knows that its only hope and expectation must be in God. Therefore, instead of discouraging the humble soul from trusting, such revelations drive it to a deeper and more utter trust. But the counterfeit humility that self-love produces plunges the soul into the depths of a faithless discouragement and drives it into the very sin with which it is so distressed.

There is an allegory that illustrates this to me wonderfully. Satan called together a council of his servants to consult how they might make a good man sin. One evil spirit started up and said, "I will make him sin." "How will you do it?" asked Satan. "I will set before him the pleasures of sin," was the reply; "I will tell him of its delights and the rich rewards it brings." "Ah," said Satan, "that will not do; he has tried it and knows better than that." Then another imp started up and said, "I will make him sin." "What will you do?" asked Satan. "I will tell him of the pains and sorrows of virtue. I will show him that virtue has no delights and brings no rewards." "Ah, no!" exclaimed Satan. "That will not do at all; for he has tried it and knows that 'Wisdom's ways *are* ways of pleasantness, and all her paths are peace.'" "Well," said another imp, starting up, "I will undertake to make him sin." "And what will you do?" asked Satan, again.

"I will discourage his soul," was the short reply. "Ah, that will do!" cried Satan. "That will do! We shall conquer him now."

An old writer says, "All discouragement is from the devil"; and I wish every Christian would take this as a motto and would realize that he must fly from discouragement as he would from sin.

But if we fail to recognize the truth about temptation, this is impossible; for if the temptations are our own fault, we cannot help being discouraged. But they are not. The Bible says, "Blessed is the man that endureth temptation"; and we are exhorted to "count it all joy when we fall into divers temptations." Temptation, therefore, cannot be sin; and the truth is, it is no more a sin to hear these whispers and suggestions of evil in our souls than it is for us to hear the wicked talk of bad men as we pass along the street. The sin comes, in either case, only by our stopping and joining in with them. If, when the wicked suggestions come, we turn from them at once, as we would from wicked talk, and pay no more attention to them than we would to the talk, we do not sin. But if we carry them on in our minds and roll them under our tongues and dwell on them with half-consent of our will to them as true, then we sin. We may be enticed by temptations a thousand times a day without sin, and we cannot help these enticings and are not to blame for them. But if we begin to think that these enticings are actual sin on our part, then the battle is half lost already, and the sin can hardly fail to gain a complete victory.

A dear lady once came to me under great darkness, simply from not understanding this. She had been living very happily in the life of faith for some time and had been so free from temptation as almost to begin to think she would never be tempted again. But suddenly a very peculiar form of temptation had assailed her, which had horrified her. She found that the moment she began to pray, dreadful thoughts of all kinds would rush into her mind. She had lived a very sheltered, innocent life; and these thoughts seemed so awful to her that she felt she must be one of the most wicked of sinners to be capable of having them. She began by thinking that she could not possibly have entered into the rest of faith and ended by concluding that she had never even been born again. Her soul was in an agony of distress. I told her that these dreadful thoughts were purely and simply temptations, and that she herself was not to blame for them at all; that she could not help them any more than she could help hearing if a wicked man should pour out his blasphemies in her presence. And I urged her to recognize and treat them as temptations only and not to blame herself or be discouraged but rather to turn at once to the Lord and commit them to Him. I showed her how great an advantage the enemy had gained by making her think these thoughts were originated by herself and by plunging her into condemnation and discouragement on account of them. And I assured her she would find a speedy victory if she would pay no attention to them but, ignoring their presence, would simply turn her back on them and look to the Lord.

She grasped the truth, and the next time these blasphemous thoughts came, she said inwardly to the enemy, "I have found you out now. It is you who are suggesting these dreadful thoughts to me, and I hate them and will have nothing to do with them. The Lord is my helper; take them to Him and settle them in His presence." Immediately the baffled enemy, finding himself discovered, fled in confusion, and her soul was perfectly delivered.

Another thing also. Our spiritual enemies know that if a Christian recognized a suggestion of evil as coming from them, he would recoil from it far more quickly than if it seems to be the suggestion of his own mind. If the devil prefaced each temptation with the words "I am the devil, your relentless enemy; I have come to make you sin," I suppose we would hardly feel any desire at all to yield to his suggestions. He has to hide himself in order to make his baits attractive. And our victory will be far more easily gained if we are not ignorant of his devices but recognize them at his very first approach.

We also make another great mistake about temptations in thinking that all time spent in combating them is lost. Hours pass, and we seem to have made no progress because we have been so beset with temptations. But it often happens that we have been serving God far more truly during these hours than in our times of comparative freedom from temptation. For we are fighting our Lord's battles when we are fighting temptation, and hours are often worth days to us under these circumstances. We read, "Blessed is the man that *endureth* temptation," and I am sure this means enduring the continuance of it and its frequent recurrence. Nothing so cultivates the grace of patience as the endurance of temptation, and nothing so drives the soul to an utter dependence upon the Lord Jesus as its continuance. And finally, nothing brings more praise and honor and glory to our Lord Himself than the trial of our faith that comes through manifold temptations. We are told that it is "more precious than of gold that perisheth, though it be tried with fire," and that we, who patiently endure the trial, shall receive for our reward "the crown of life, which the Lord hath promised to them that love him."

We cannot wonder, therefore, any longer at the exhortation with which the Holy Ghost opens the Book of James: "Count it all joy when ye fall into divers temptations; knowing this, that the trying of your faith worketh patience. But let patience have her perfect work, that ye may be perfect and entire, wanting nothing."

Temptation is plainly one of the instruments used by God to complete our perfection; and thus sin's own weapons are turned against itself, and we see how it is that all things, even temptations, can work together for good to them that love God.

As to the way of victory over temptation, it seems hardly necessary to say to those whom I am at this time especially addressing that it is to be by faith; for this is, of course, the foundation upon which the whole interior life rests. Our one great motto is throughout, "We are nothing: Christ is all"; and always and everywhere we have started out to stand and walk and overcome and live by faith. We have discovered our own utter helplessness and know that we cannot do anything for ourselves; and we have learned that our only way, therefore, is to hand the temptation over to our Lord and trust Him to conquer it for us. But when we put it into His hands, we must *leave* it there. The greatest difficulty of all is, I think, this *leaving*. It seems impossible to believe that the Lord can or will manage our temptations without our help, especially if they do not immediately disappear. To go on patiently "enduring" the continuance of a temptation without yielding to it and also without snatching ourselves out of the Lord's hands in regard to it is a wonderful victory for our impatient natures, but it is a victory we must gain if we would do what will please God.

We must then commit ourselves as really to the Lord for victory over our temptations as we committed ourselves at first for forgiveness; and we must leave ourselves just as utterly in His hands for one as for the other.

Thousands of God's children have done this and can testify today that marvelous victories have been gained for them over numberless temptations, and that they have in very truth been made "more than conquerors" through Him who loves them.

But into this part of the subject I cannot go at present, as my object has been rather to present temptation in its true light than to develop the way of victory over it. I desire greatly that conscientious, faithful souls should be delivered from the bondage into which they are sure to be brought if they fail to understand the true nature and use of temptation and confound it with sin. When temptation is recognized *as* temptation, we shall be able to say at once, "Get thee behind me"; and shall walk even through the midst of the fiercest assaults with unclouded and triumphant peace; knowing that, "when the enemy shall come in like a flood, the Spirit of the LORD shall lift up a standard against him."

Chapter 11

Difficulties Concerning Failures

The very title of this chapter may perhaps startle some. "Failures. . ." they will say. "We thought there were no failures in this life of faith!"

To this I would answer that there ought not to be and need not be; but, as a fact, there sometimes are, and we must deal with the facts and not with theories. No safe teacher of this interior life ever says that it becomes impossible to sin; they only insist that sin ceases to be a necessity, and that a possibility of continual victory is opened before us. And there are very few, if any, who do not confess that, as to their own actual experience, they have at times been overcome by at least a momentary temptation.

Of course, in speaking of sin here, I mean conscious, known sin. I do not touch on the subject of sins of ignorance, or what is called the inevitable sin of our nature, which are all met by the provisions of Christ and do not disturb our fellowship with God. I have no desire nor ability to treat of the doctrines concerning sin; these I will leave with the theologians to discuss and settle, while I speak only of the believer's experience in the matter.

There are many things which we do innocently enough

until an increasing light shows them to be wrong, and these may all be classed under sins of ignorance; but because they are done in ignorance they do not bring us under condemnation and do not come within the range of the present discussion.

An illustration of this occurred once in my presence. A little baby girl was playing about the library one warm summer afternoon, while her father was resting on the lounge. A pretty inkstand on the table took the child's fancy and, unnoticed by any one, she climbed on a chair and secured it. Then, walking over to her father with an air of childish triumph, she turned it upside down on the white expanse of his shirt bosom and laughed with glee as she saw the black streams trickling down on every side.

This was a very wrong thing for the child to do, but it could not be called sin, for she knew no better. Had she been older and been made to understand that inkstands were not playthings, it would have been sin. "To him that knoweth to do good, and doeth it not, to him it is sin"; and in all I shall say concerning sin in this chapter, I desire it to be fully understood that I have reference simply to that which comes within the range of our consciousness.

Misunderstandings, then, on this point of known or conscious sin, opens the way for great dangers in the life of faith. When a believer, who has, as he trusts, entered upon the highway of holiness, finds himself surprised into sin, he is tempted either to be utterly discouraged and to give everything up as lost; or else in order to preserve the doctrines untouched, he feels it necessary to cover his sin up, calling it infirmity and refusing to be candid and aboveboard about it. Either of these courses is equally fatal to any real growth and progress in the life of holiness. The only way is to face the sad fact at once, call the thing by its right name, and discover, if possible, the reason and the remedy.

This life of union with God requires the utmost honesty with Him and with ourselves. The blessing that the sin itself would only momentarily disturb is sure to be lost by any dishonest dealing with it.

A sudden failure is no reason for being discouraged and giving up all as lost. Neither is the integrity of our doctrine touched by it. We are not preaching a *state*, but a *walk*. The highway of holiness is not a *place*, but a *way*. Sanctification is not a thing to be picked up at a certain stage of our experience and forever after possessed, but it is a life to be lived day by day and hour by hour. We may for a moment turn aside from a path, but the path is not obliterated by our wandering and can be instantly regained. And in this life and walk of faith, there may be momentary failures that, although very sad and greatly to be deplored, need not, if rightly met, disturb the attitude of the soul as to entire consecration and perfect trust, nor interrupt, for more than the passing moment, its happy communion with its Lord.

The great point is an instant return to God. Our sin is no reason for ceasing to trust but only an unanswerable argument why we must trust more fully than ever. From whatever cause we have been betrayed into failure, it is very certain that there is no remedy to be found in discouragement. As well might a child who is learning to walk, lie down in despair when he has fallen and refuse to take another step, as a believer, who is seeking to learn how to live and walk by faith give up in despair because of having fallen into sin. The only way in both cases is to get right up and try again. When the children of Israel had met with that disastrous defeat, soon after their entrance into the land, before the little city of Ai, they were all so utterly discouraged that we read: "Wherefore the hearts of the people melted, and became as water. And Joshua rent his clothes, and fell to the earth upon his face before the ark of the LORD until the eventide, he and the elders of Israel, and put dust upon their heads. And Joshua said, Alas, O Lord GOD, wherefore hast thou at all brought this people over Jordan, to deliver us into the hand of the Amorites, to destroy us? would to God we had been content, and dwelt on the other side Jordan! O Lord, what shall I say, when Israel turneth their backs before their enemies! For the Canaanites and all the inhabitants of the land shall hear of it, and shall environ us round, and cut off our name from the earth: and what wilt thou do unto thy great name?"

What a wail of despair this was! And how exactly it is repeated by many a child of God in the present day, whose heart, because of a defeat, melts and becomes as water, and who cries out, "Would to God we had been content, and dwelt on the other side Jordan!" and predicts for itself further failures and even utter discomfiture before its enemies. No doubt Joshua thought then, as we are apt to think now, that discouragement and despair were the only proper and safe condition after such a failure. But God thought otherwise. "And the LORD said unto Joshua, Get thee up; wherefore liest thou thus upon thy face?" The proper thing to do was not to abandon themselves thus to utter discouragement, humble as it might look, but at once to face the evil and get rid of it, and afresh and immediately to "sanctify themselves."

"Up, sanctify the people" is always God's command. "Lie down and be discouraged" is always our temptation. Our feeling is that it is presumptuous, and even almost impertinent, to go at once to the Lord after having sinned against Him. It seems as if we ought to suffer the consequences of our sin first for a little while and endure the accusings of our conscience; and we can hardly believe that the Lord *can* be willing at once to receive us back into loving fellowship with Himself.

A little girl once expressed this feeling to me with a child's outspoken candor. She had asked whether the Lord Jesus always forgave us for our sins as soon as we asked Him, and I had said, "Yes, of course He does." "*Just* as soon?" she repeated doubtingly. "Yes," I replied, "the very minute we ask, He forgives us." "Well," she said deliberately, "I cannot believe that. I should think He would make us feel sorry for two or three days first. And then I should think He would make us ask Him a great many times and in a very pretty way, too, not just in common talk. And I believe that *is* the way He does, and you need not try to make me think He forgives me right at once, no matter what the Bible says." She only *said* what most Christians *think,* and what is worse, what most Christians act on, making their discouragement and their very remorse separate them infinitely further off from God than their sin would have done. Yet it is so totally contrary to the way we like our children to act toward us that I wonder how we ever could have conceived such an idea of God. How a mother grieves when a naughty child goes off alone in despairing remorse and doubts her willingness to forgive; and how, on the other hand, her whole heart goes out in welcoming love to the repentant little one who runs to her at once and begs her forgiveness! Surely our God felt this yearning love when He said to us, "Return, ye backsliding children, and I will heal your backslidings."

The fact is that the same moment which brings the consciousness of sin ought to bring also the confession and the consciousness of forgiveness. This is especially essential to an unwavering walk in the "life hid with Christ in God," for no separation from Him can be tolerated here for an instant.

We can only walk this path by "looking continually unto Jesus," moment by moment; and if our eyes are turned away from Him to look upon our own sin and our own weakness, we shall leave the path at once. The believer, therefore, who has, as he trusts, entered upon this highway, if he finds himself overcome by sin, must flee with it instantly to the Lord. He must act on 1 John 1:9, "If we confess our sins, he is faithful and just to forgive us our sins, and to cleanse us from all unrighteousness." He must not hide his sin and seek to salve it over with excuses or to push it out of his memory by the lapse of time. But he must do as the children of Israel did, rise up "*early* in the morning," and "*run*" to the place where the evil thing is hidden and take it out of its hiding place, and lay it "out before the Lord." He must confess his sin. And then he must stone it with stones and burn it with fire and utterly put it away from him and raise over it a great heap of stones that it may be forever hidden from his sight. And he must believe, then and there, that God *is,* according to His word, faithful and just to forgive him his sin, and that He does do it; and further, that He also cleanses him from all unrighteousness. He must claim by faith an immediate forgiveness and an immediate cleansing and must go on trusting harder and more absolutely than ever.

As soon as Israel's sin had been brought to light and put away, at once God's word came again in a message of glorious encouragement: "Fear not, neither be thou dismayed. . .see, I have given into thy hand the king of Ai, and his people, and his city, and his land." Our courage must rise higher than ever, and we must abandon ourselves more completely to the Lord that His mighty power may the more perfectly work in us "all the good pleasure of His will." Moreover, we must forget our sin as soon as it is thus confessed and forgiven. We must not dwell on it and examine it and indulge in a luxury of distress and remorse. We must not put it on a pedestal and then walk around it and view it on every side and so magnify it into a mountain that hides God from our eyes. We must follow the example of Paul, and, "forgetting those things which are behind, and reaching forth unto those things which are before," we must "press toward the mark for the prize of the high calling of God in Christ Jesus."

Let me recall two contrasting illustrations of these things. One was an earnest Christian man, an active worker in the church, who had been living for several months in an experience of great peace and joy. He was suddenly overcome by a temptation to treat a brother unkindly. Having supposed it to be an impossibility that he could ever so sin again, he was plunged at once into the deepest discouragement and concluded he had been altogether mistaken and had never entered into the life of full trust at all. Day by day his discouragement increased until it became despair, and he concluded at last that he had never even been born again and gave himself up for lost. He spent three years of utter misery going farther and farther away from God and being gradually drawn off into one sin after another until his life was a curse to himself and to all around him. His health failed under the terrible burden, and fears were entertained for his reason. At the end of three years he met a Christian lady who understood this truth about sin that I have been trying to explain. In a few moments' conversation she found out his trouble and at once said, "You sinned in that act; there is no doubt about it, and I do not want you to try to excuse it. But have you never confessed it to the Lord and asked Him to forgive you?" "Confessed it!" he exclaimed. "Why, it seems to me I have done nothing but confess it and entreat God to forgive me, night and day, for all these three dreadful years." "And you have never believed He did forgive you?" asked the lady. "No," said the poor man, "how could I, for I never *felt* as if He did?" "But suppose He had said He forgave you, would not that have done as well as for you to feel it?" "Oh yes," replied the man. "If God said it, of course I would believe it." "Very well, He does say so," was the lady's answer; and she turned to the verse we have taken above (1 John 1:9) and read it aloud. "Now," she continued, "you have been all these three years confessing and confessing your sin, and all the while God's record has been declaring that He was faithful and just to forgive it and to cleanse you, and yet you have never once believed it. You have been 'making God a liar' all this while by refusing to believe His record."

The poor man saw the whole thing and was dumb with amazement and consternation; and when the lady proposed that they should kneel down, and that he should confess his past unbelief and sin and should claim, then and there, a present forgiveness and a present cleansing, he obeyed like one in a maze. But the result was glorious. The light broke in, his darkness vanished, and he began aloud to praise God for the wonderful deliverance. In a few minutes his soul was enabled to traverse back by faith the whole long weary journey that he had been three years in making, and he found himself once more resting in the Lord and rejoicing in the fullness of His salvation.

The other illustration was the case of a Christian lady who had been living in the land of promise a few weeks and who had had a very bright and victorious experience. Suddenly at the end of that time, she was overcome by a violent burst of anger. For a moment a flood of discouragement swept over her soul. The temptation came, "There now, that shows it was all a mistake. Of course you have been deceived about the whole thing and have never entered into the life of faith at all. And now you may as well give up altogether, for you never can consecrate yourself any more entirely nor trust any more fully than you did this time; so it is very plain this life of holiness is not for you!" These thoughts flashed through her mind in a moment; but she was well taught in the ways of God, and she said at once, "Yes, I have sinned, and it is very sad. But the Bible says that, if we confess our sins, God is faithful and just to forgive us our sins, and to cleanse us from all unrighteousness; and I believe He will do it." She did not delay a moment but, while still boiling over with anger, she ran (for she could not walk) into a room where she could be alone, and kneeling down beside the bed she said, "Lord, I confess my sin. I have sinned; I am even at this very moment sinning. I hate it, but I cannot get rid of it. I confess it with shame and confusion of face to thee. And now I believe that, according to Thy word, Thou dost forgive and Thou dost cleanse." She said it out loud, for the inward turmoil was too great for it to be said inside. As the words "Thou dost forgive and Thou does cleanse" passed her lips, the deliverance came. The Lord said, "Peace, be still!" and there was a great calm. A flood of light and joy burst on her soul, the enemy fled, and she was more than conqueror through Him that loved her. The whole thing, the sin and the recovery from it, had occupied not five minutes, and her feet trod more firmly than ever in the blessed highway of holiness. Thus the "valley of Achor" became to her a "door of hope," and she sang afresh and with deeper meaning her song of deliverance, "I will sing unto the Lord, for He hath triumphed gloriously."

The truth is, the only remedy, after all, in every emergency, is to trust in the Lord. And if this is all we ought to do and all we can do, is it not better to do at it once? I have often been brought to a stand by the question, "Well, what *can* I do but trust?" And I have realized at once the folly of seeking for deliverance in any other way, by saying to myself, "I shall have to come to simple trusting in the end, and why not come to it at once, now in the beginning." It is a life and walk of *faith* we have entered upon; and if we fail in it, our only recovery must lie in an increase of faith, not in a lessening of it.

Let every failure then, if any occur, drive you instantly to the Lord with a more complete abandonment and a more perfect trust; and if you do this, you will find that, sad as it is, your failure has not taken you out of the land of rest nor broken for long your sweet communion with Him.

Where failure is thus met, a recurrence is far more likely to be prevented than where the soul allows itself to pass through a season of despair and remorse. If it should however sometimes recur, and is always similarly treated, it is sure to become less and less frequent, until finally it ceases altogether. There are some happy souls who learn the whole lesson at once; but the blessing is also upon those who take slower steps and gain a more gradual victory.

Having shown the way of deliverance from failure, I would now say a little as to the causes of failure in this life of full salvation. The causes do not lie in the strength of the temptation, nor in our own weakness, nor above all in any lack in the power or willingness of our Savior to save us. The promise to Israel was positive: "There shall not any man be able to stand before thee all the days of thy life." And the promise to us is equally positive: "God is faithful, who will not suffer you to be tempted above that ye are able; but will with the temptation also make a way to escape, that ye may be able to bear it." The men of Ai were "but few," and yet the people who had conquered the mighty Jericho "fled before the men of Ai." It was not the strength of their enemy, neither had God failed them. The cause of their defeat lay somewhere else, and the Lord Himself declares it: "Israel hath sinned, and they have also transgressed my covenant which I commanded them: for they have even taken of the accursed thing, and have also stolen, and dissembled also, and they have put it even among their own stuff. Therefore the children of Israel could not stand before

their enemies, but turned their backs before their enemies."
It was a hidden evil that conquered them. Buried under the
earth, in an obscure tent in that vast army, was hidden
something against which God had a controversy; and this
little hidden thing made the whole army helpless before
their enemies. "There is an accursed thing in the midst of
thee, O Israel: thou canst not stand before thine enemies,
until ye take away the accursed thing from among you."

The lesson here is simply this, that anything cherished
in the heart which is contrary to the will of God, let it seem
ever so insignificant or be ever so deeply hidden, will cause
us to fall before our enemies. Any conscious root of bitterness cherished toward another, any self-seeking, any harsh
judgments, any slackness in obeying the voice of the Lord,
and doubtful habits or surroundings—these things or any
one of them, consciously indulged, will effectually cripple
and paralyze our spiritual life. We may have hidden the evil
in the most remote corner of our hearts and may have covered it over from our sight, refusing even to recognize its
existence, although we cannot help being all the time
secretly aware that it is there. We may steadily ignore it and
persist in declarations of consecration and full trust; we
may be more earnest than ever in our religious duties and
have the eyes of our understanding opened more and more
to the truth and the beauty of the life and walk of faith. We
may seem to ourselves and to others to have reached an
almost impregnable position of victory, and yet we may
find ourselves suffering bitter defeats. We may wonder and
question and despair and pray. Nothing will do any good
until the wrong thing is dug up from its hiding place,
brought out to the light, and laid before God.

The moment, therefore, that a believer who is walking
in this interior life meets with a defeat, he must at once seek
for the cause, not in the strength of that particular enemy,

but in something behind—some hidden want of consecration lying at the very center of his being. Just as a headache is not the disease itself, but only a symptom of a disease, situated in some other part of the body, so the failure in such a Christian is only the symptom of an evil, hidden in probably a very different part of his nature.

Sometimes the evil may be hidden even in what at a cursory glance would look like good. Beneath apparent zeal for the truth may be hidden a judging spirit or a subtle leaning to our own understanding. Beneath apparent Christian faithfulness may be hidden an absence of Christian love. Beneath an apparently rightful care for our affairs may be hidden a great want to trust in God. I believe our blessed guide, the indwelling Holy Spirit, is always secretly discovering these things to us by continual little checks and pangs of conscience so that we are left without excuse. But it is very easy to disregard His gentle voice and insist upon it to ourselves that all is right while the fatal evil continues hidden in our midst causing defeat in most unexpected quarters.

A capital illustration of this occurred to me once in my housekeeping. We had moved into a new house and, in looking over it to see if it was all ready for occupancy, I noticed in the cellar a very clean-looking cider cask headed up at both ends. I debated with myself whether I should have it taken out of the cellar and opened to see what was in it but concluded, as it seemed empty and looked clean, to leave it undisturbed, especially as it would have been quite a piece of work to get it up the stairs. I did not feel quite easy but reasoned away my scruples and left it. Every spring and fall, when housecleaning time came on, I would remember that cask with a little twinge of my housewifely conscience, feeling I could not quite rest in the thought of a perfectly clean house while it remained unopened, as how did I know but under its fair exterior it contained some hidden evil? Still

I managed to quiet my scruples on the subject, thinking always of the trouble it would involve to investigate it; and for two or three years the innocent-looking cask stood quietly in our cellar. Then, most unaccountably, moths began to fill our house. I used every possible precaution against them and made every effort to eradicate them but in vain. They increased rapidly and threatened to ruin everything we had. I suspected our carpets as being the cause and subjected them to a thorough cleaning. I suspected our furniture and had it newly upholstered. I suspected all sorts of impossible things. At last the thought of the cask flashed on me. At once I had it brought up out of the cellar and the head knocked in, and I think it safe to say that thousands of moths poured out. The previous occupant of the house must have headed it up with something in it which bred moths, and this was the cause of all my trouble.

Now, I believe that, in the same way, some innocent-looking habit or indulgence, some apparently unimportant and safe thing, about which, however, we have now and then little twinges of conscience—something which is not brought out fairly into the light and investigated under the searching eye of God—lies at the root of most of the failure in this interior life. *All* is not given up. Some secret corner is kept locked against the entrance of the Lord. Some evil thing is hidden in the recesses of our hearts and, therefore, we cannot stand before our enemies but find ourselves smitten down in their presence.

In order to prevent failure or to discover its cause if we find we have failed, it is necessary to keep continually before us this prayer: "Search me, O God, and know my heart; try me, and know my thoughts: and see if there be any wicked way in me, and lead me in the way everlasting."

Let me beg of you, however, dear Christians, do not think because I have said all this about failure that I believe in it. There is no necessity for it whatever. The Lord Jesus *is* able, according to the declaration concerning Him, to deliver us out of the hands of our enemies that we may "serve Him without fear, in holiness and righteousness before Him, all the days of our life." Let us then pray, every one of us, day and night, "Lord, keep us from sinning, and make us living witnesses of thy mighty power to save to the uttermost"; and let us never be satisfied until we are so pliable in His hands and have learned so to trust Him that He will be able to "make [us] perfect in every good work to do his will, working in [us] that which is well pleasing in his sight, through Jesus Christ; to whom be glory for ever and ever. Amen."

Chapter 12

Is God in Everything?

One of the greatest obstacles to an unwavering experience in the interior life is the difficulty of seeing God in everything. People say, "I can easily submit to things that come from God; but I cannot submit to man, and most of my trials and crosses come through human instrumentality." Or they say, "It is all well enough to talk of trusting; but when I commit a matter to God, man is sure to come in and disarrange it all; and while I have no difficulty in trusting God, I do see serious difficulties in the way of trusting men."

This is no imaginary trouble but is of vital importance; and if it cannot be met, it does really make the life of faith an impossible and visionary theory. For nearly everything in life comes to us through human instrumentalities, and most of our trials are the result of somebody's failure or ignorance or carelessness or sin. We know God cannot be the author of these things; and yet, unless He is the agent in the matter, how can we say to Him about it, "Thy will be done?"

Besides, what good is there in trusting our affairs to God, if, after all, man is to be allowed to come in and disarrange them; and how is it possible to live by faith if human agencies, in whom it would be wrong and foolish to trust, are to have a prevailing influence in molding our lives?

Moreover, things in which we can see God's hand always have a sweetness in them that consoles while it wounds; but the trials inflicted by man are full of nothing but bitterness.

What is needed, then, is to see God in everything and to receive everything directly from His hands with no intervention of second causes; and it is to just this that we must be brought before we can know an abiding experience of entire abandonment and perfect trust. Our abandonment must be to God, not to man; and our trust must be in Him, not in any arm of flesh, or we shall fail at the first trial.

The question here confronts us at once, "But is God in everything, and have we any warrant from the scripture for receiving everything from His hands without regarding the second causes that may have been instrumental in bringing them about?" I answer to this, unhesitatingly, Yes. To the children of God, everything comes directly from their Father's hand, no matter who or what may have been the apparent agents. There are no "second causes" for them.

The whole teaching of scripture asserts and implies this. Not a sparrow falls to the ground without our Father. The very hairs of our head are all numbered. We are not to be careful about anything because our Father cares for us. We are not to avenge ourselves because our Father has charged Himself with our defense. We are not to fear for the Lord is on our side. No one can be against us because He is for us. We shall not want for He is our Shepherd. When we pass through the rivers they shall not overflow us, and when we walk through the fire we shall not be burned because He will be with us. He shuts the mouths of lions that they cannot hurt us. "He delivereth and rescueth." "He changeth the times and the seasons: he removeth kings, and setteth up kings." A man's heart is in His hand, and, "as the rivers of water, he turneth it whithersoever he will." He ruleth over all the kingdoms of the heathen; and in His hand there is power and might, "so that none is able to withstand" Him. He "rulest the raging of the sea; when the waves thereof arise, he stilleth them." He "bringeth the counsel of the heathen to naught: he maketh the devices of the people of none effect." "Whatsoever the Lord pleased, that did he in heaven, and in earth, in the seas, and all deep places." "Lo, these are parts of his ways: but how little a portion is heard of him? but the thunder of his power who can understand?" "Hast thou not known? hast thou not heard, that the ever-lasting God, the LORD, the Creator of the ends of the earth, fainteth not, neither is weary? there is no searching of his understanding."

And it is this very God who is declared to be "our refuge and strength, a very present help in trouble. Therefore will not we fear, though the earth be removed, and though the mountains be carried into the midst of the sea; though the waters thereof roar and be troubled, though the mountains shake with the swelling thereof." "I will say of the LORD, He is my refuge and my fortress: my God; in him will I trust. Surely he shall deliver thee from the snare of the fowler, and from the noisome pestilence. He shall cover thee with his feathers, and under his wings shalt thou trust: his truth shall be thy shield and buckler. Thou shalt not be afraid for the terror by night; nor for the arrow that flieth by day; nor for the pestilence that walketh in darkness; nor for the destruction that wasteth at noonday. A thousand shall fall at thy side, and ten thousand at thy right hand; but it shall not come nigh thee. . . . Because thou has made the LORD, which is my refuge, even the most High, thy habitation; there shall no evil befall thee, neither shall any plague come nigh thy dwelling. For he shall give his angels charge over thee, to keep thee in all thy ways." "Be content with such things as ye have: for he hath said, I will never leave thee, nor forsake thee. So that we may boldy say, The Lord is my helper, and I will not fear what man shall do unto me."

To my own mind, these scriptures, and many others like them, settle forever the question as to the power of "second causes" in the life of the children of God. Second causes must all be under the control of our Father, and not one of them can touch us except with His knowledge and by His permission. It may be the sin of man that originates the action and, therefore, the thing itself cannot be said to be the will of God; but by the time it reaches us it has become God's will for us and must be accepted as directly from His hands. No man or company of men, no power in earth or heaven can touch that soul which is abiding in Christ without first passing through His encircling presence and receiving the seal of His permission. If God be for us, it matters not who may be against us; nothing can disturb or harm us except He shall see that it is best for us and shall stand aside to let it pass.

An earthly parent's care for his helpless child is a feeble illustration of this. If the child is in its father's arms, nothing can touch it without the father's consent unless he is too weak to prevent it. And even if this should be the case, he suffers the harm first in his own person before he allows it to reach his child. If an earthly parent would thus care for his little helpless one, how much more will our heavenly Father, whose love is infinitely greater and whose strength and wisdom can never be baffled, care for us! I am afraid there are some, even of God's own children, who scarcely think that He is equal to themselves in tenderness and love and thoughtful care; and who, in their secret thoughts, charge Him with a neglect and indifference of which they would feel themselves incapable. The truth really is that His care is infinitely superior to any possibilities of human care and that He, who counts the very hairs of our heads and suffers not a sparrow to fall without Him, takes note of the minutest matters that can affect the lives of His children and regulates them all according to His own perfect will, let their origin be what they may.

The instances of this are numberless. Take Joseph. What could have seemed more apparently on the face of it to be the result of sin and utterly contrary to the will of God than the action of his brethren in selling him into slavery? And yet Joseph, in speaking of it, said, "As for you, ye thought evil against me; but God meant it unto good." "Now therefore be not grieved, nor angry with yourselves, that ye sold me hither: for God did send me before you to preserve life." It was undoubtedly sin in Joseph's brethren, but by the time it had reached Joseph it had become God's will for him and was, in truth, though he did not see it then, the greatest blessing of his whole life. And thus we see how God can make even "the wrath of man to praise Him," and how all things, even the sins of others, "shall work together for good to them that love God."

I learned this lesson practically and experimentally long years before I knew the scriptural truth concerning it. I was attending a prayer meeting held in the interests of the life of faith when a strange lady rose to speak, and I looked at her, wondering who she could be, little thinking she was to bring a message to my soul which would teach me a grand practical lesson. She said she had great difficulty in living the life of faith on account of the second causes that seemed to her to control nearly everything that concerned her. Her perplexity became so great that at last she began to ask God to teach her the truth about it, whether He really was in everything or not. After praying this for a few days, she had what she described as a vision. She thought she was in a perfectly dark place, and that there advanced toward her, from a distance, a body of light which gradually surrounded and enveloped her and everything around her. As it approached, a voice seemed to say, "This is the presence of God! This is the presence of God!" While surrounded with this presence, all the great and awful things in life seemed to pass before her—fighting armies, wicked men, raging beasts, storms and pestilences, sin and suffering of every kind. She shrunk back at first in terror; but she soon saw that the presence of God so surrounded and enveloped herself and each one of these things, that not a lion could reach out its paw, nor a bullet fly through the air, except as the presence of God moved out of the way to permit it. And she saw that if there were ever so thin a film, as it were, of this glorious presence between herself and the most terrible violence, not a hair of her head could be ruffled, nor anything touch her, except as the presence divided to let the evil through. Then all the small and annoying things of life passed before her; and equally she saw that there also she was so enveloped in this presence of God, that not a cross look, nor a harsh word, nor petty trial of any kind could affect her, unless God's encircling presence moved out of the way to let it.

Her difficulty vanished. Her question was answered forever. God *was* in everything; and to her henceforth there were no second causes. She saw that her life came to her, day by day and hour by hour, directly from the hand of God, let the agencies which should seem to control it be what they might. And never again had she found any difficulty in an abiding consent to His will, in an unwavering trust in His care.

Would that it were only possible to make every Christian see this truth as plainly as I see it! For I am convinced it is the only clue to a completely restful life. Nothing else will enable a soul to live only in the present moment, as we are commanded to do, and to take no thought for the morrow. Nothing else will take all the risks and "supposes" out of a Christian's life and enable him to say, "Surely goodness and mercy shall follow me all the days of my life." Under God's care we run no risks. I once heard of a poor woman who earned a precarious living by daily labor, but who was a joyous, triumphant Christian. "Ah, Nancy," said a gloomy Christian lady to her one day, who almost disapproved of her constant cheerfulness and yet envied it—"Ah, Nancy, it is all well enough to be happy now, but I should think the thoughts of your future would sober you. Only suppose, for instance, that you should have a spell of sickness and be unable to work; or suppose your present employers should move away, and no one else should give you anything to do; or suppose—" "Stop!" cried Nancy, "I never supposes. De Lord is my shepherd, and I knows I shall not want. And, honey," she added to her gloomy friend, "it's all dem *supposes* as is makin' you so mis'able. You'd better give dem all up and just trust de Lord."

Nothing else but this seeing God in everything will make us loving and patient with those who annoy and trouble us. They will be to us then only the instruments for accomplishing His tender and wise purposes toward us, and we shall even find ourselves at last inwardly thanking them for the blessings they bring.

Nothing else will completely put an end to all murmuring or rebelling thoughts. Christians often feel at liberty to murmur against man when they would not dare to murmur against God. Therefore, this way of receiving things would make it impossible ever to murmur. If our Father permits a trial to come, it must be because the trial is the sweetest and best thing that could happen to us, and we must accept it with thanks from His dear hand. This does not mean, however, that we must like or enjoy the trial itself, but that we must like God's will in the trial; and it is not hard to do this when we have learned to know that His will is the will of love and is, therefore, always lovely.

A good illustration of this may be found in the familiar fact of a mother giving medicine to her dearly loved child. The bottle *holds* the medicine, but the mother *gives* it; and the bottle is not responsible, but the mother. No matter how full her closet may be of bottles of medicine, the mother will not allow one drop to be given to the child unless she believes it will be good for him; but when she does believe it will be good for her darling, the very depth of her love compels her to force it on the child, no matter how bitter may be its taste.

The human beings around us are often the bottles that hold our medicine, but it is our Father's hand of love that pours out the medicine and compels us to drink it. The human bottle is the "second cause" of our trial; but it has no real agency in it, for the medicine that these human "bottles" hold is prescribed for us and given to us by the Great Physician of our souls who is seeking thereby to heal all our spiritual diseases.

For instance, I know no better medicine to cure the disease of irritability than to be compelled to live with a human "bottle" of sensitiveness, whom we are bound to consider and yield to.

Shall we rebel against the human bottles then? Shall we not rather take thankfully from our Father's hand the medicine they contain, and, losing sight of the second cause, say joyfully, "Thy will be done," in everything that comes to us, no matter what its source may be?

This way of seeing our Father in everything makes life one long thanksgiving and gives a rest of heart and, more than that, a gaiety of spirit that is unspeakable.

Faber says, in his wonderful hymn on the will of God—

> *I know not what it is to doubt,*
> *My heart is always gay;*

I run no risks, for, come what will,
*   Thou always hast Thy way.*

Since, therefore, God is sure to have His own way concerning those who abandon themselves to Him in perfect trust, into what wonderful green pastures of inward rest and beside what blessedly still waters of inward refreshment will He lead all such!

If the will of God is our will, and if He always has His way, then we always have our way also, and we reign in a perpetual kingdom. He who sides with God cannot fail to win in every encounter; and whether the result shall be joy or sorrow, failure or success, death or life, we may under all circumstances join in the apostle's shout of victory, "Thanks be unto God, which always causeth us to triumph in Christ!"

THE WILL OF GOD*

Thou sweet, beloved Will of God,
*   My anchor ground, my fortress hill,*
My spirit's silent, fair abode,
*   In Thee I hide me and am still.*

O Will, that willest good alone,
*   Lead Thou the way, Thou guidest best;*
A little child I follow on,
*   And trusting lean upon the breast.*

Thy beautiful, sweet Will, my God,
*   Holds fast in its sublime embrace*
My captive will, a gladsome bird,
*   Prisoned in such a realm of grace.*

Within this place of certain good,
  Love ever more expands her wings;
Or, nestling in Thy perfect choice,
  Abides content with what it brings.

Oh, sweetest burden, lightest yoke,
  It lifts, it bears my happy soul,
It giveth wings to this poor heart;
  My freedom is Thy grand control.

Upon God's Will I lay me down,
  As child upon its mother's breast;
No silken couch, nor softest bed,
  Could ever give me such sweet rest.

Thy wonderful, grand Will, my God,
  With triumph now, I make it mine,
And Love shall cry a jealous Yes,
  To every dear command of Thine.

*From "Hymns of Consecration"

PART III
RESULTS

Chapter 13

Bondage or Liberty

It is a fact beyond question that there are two kinds of Christian experience, one of which is an experience of bondage and the other an experience of liberty.

In the first case the soul is controlled by a stern sense of duty and obeys the laws of God, either from fear of punishment or from expectation of wages. In the other case the controlling power is an inward life-principle that works out, by the force of its own motions or instincts, the will of the divine life-giver without fear of punishment or hope of reward. In the first the Christian is a servant and works for hire; in the second he is a son and works for love.

There ought not, it is true, to be this contrast in the experience of Christians, for to "walk at liberty" is plainly their only right and normal condition; but as we have to deal with what is, rather than with what ought to be, we cannot shut our eyes to the sad condition of bondage in which so many of God's children pass a large part of their Christian lives. The reason of this and the remedy for it are not difficult to find. The reason is legality, and the remedy is Christ.

Nowhere do we find those two forms or stages of Christian life more fully developed and contrasted than in the epistle to the Galatians. The occasion of its being written was that some Jewish brethren had come among the churches in Galatia and, by representing that certain forms and ceremonies were necessary to their salvation, had tried to draw them away from the liberty of the gospel. And with these teachers Peter had allowed himself to unite. Therefore Paul reproves, not only the Galatians, but also Peter himself.

Neither Peter nor the Galatians had committed any moral sin; but they had committed a spiritual sin. They had gotten into a wrong attitude of soul toward God—a legal attitude. They had begun, as Christians generally do, in the right attitude; that is, they had entered by the "hearing of faith" into the spiritual life. But when it came to a question of how they were to live in this life, they had changed their ground. They had sought to substitute works for faith. Having "begun in the Spirit," they were now seeking to be "made perfect by the flesh." They had, in short, descended, in their Christian living, from the plane of life to the plane of law.

An illustration will help us to understand this. Here are two men who neither of them steal. Outwardly their actions are equally honest, but inwardly there is a vital difference. One man has a dishonest nature that wants to steal and is only deterred by the fear of a penalty while the other possesses an honest nature that hates thieving and could not be induced to steal, even by the hope of a reward. The one is honest in the spirit; the other is honest only in the flesh. No words are needed to say of which sort the Christian life is meant to be.

We are, however, continually tempted to forget that it is not what men *do* that is the vital matter but rather what they *are*. In Christ Jesus neither legal observances avail anything nor the omission of legal observances, "but a new creature." God is a great deal more concerned about our really *being* "new creatures" than about anything else because He knows that if we *are* right as to our inward being, we shall certainly *do* right as to our outward actions. We may, in fact, sometimes even *do* right without *being* right at all; and it is very evident that no doing of this kind has any vitality in it nor is of any real account. The essential thing, therefore, is character, and *doing* is valuable only as it is an indication of *being*.

Paul was grieved with the Galatian Christians because they seemed to have lost sight of this vital truth, that the inward life, the "new creature," was the only thing that availed. They had begun on this plane, but they had "fallen from grace" to a lower plane, where the "oldness of the letter" was put in place of the "newness of the spirit." "Christ is become of no effect unto you, whosoever of you are justified by the law; ye are fallen from grace."

This passage is the only one in which the expression "fallen from grace" is used in the New Testament; and it means that the Galatians had made the mistake of thinking that something else besides Christ was necessary for their right Christian living. The Jewish brethren who had come among them had taught them that Christ alone was not enough, but that obedience to the ceremonial law must be added.

They had, therefore, imported, as being necessary for salvation, some ceremonies out of the Jewish ritual and had tried to compel the "Gentiles to live as do the Jews." Modern Christians are greatly surprised at them and wonder how they could have been so legal. But is there not the same temptation to legality, under a different form, among these same modern Christians? *They* added the ceremonial law; *we* add resolutions or agonizings or Christian work or church-going or religious ceremonies of one sort or another; and what is there, therefore, to choose between us and them? It does not make much difference what you add; the wrong thing is to add anything at all.

We are full of condemnation of the "Jew's religion," because it "frustrates the grace of God" and makes Christ to be "dead in vain," by depending upon outward deeds and outward ceremonies to bring salvation. But I fear there is a great deal of the "Jew's religion" mixed up with the Christian religion now, just as there was among these Galatian Christians and that the grace of God is as much frustrated by our legality as by theirs, although ours may manifest itself in a slightly different form.

The following contrasts may help some to understand the difference between these two kinds of religion and may also enable them to discover where the secret of their own experience of legal bondage lies:

> The law says, This *do,* and thou shalt live.
> The gospel says, *Live,* and then thou shalt do.

> The law says, *Pay* me that thou owest.
> The gospel says, I frankly *forgive* thee all.

> The law says, *Make* you a new heart and a new spirit.
> The gospel says, A new heart will I *give* you, and a
> new spirit will I put within you.

> The law says, Thou shalt love the LORD thy God
> with all thine heart, and with all thy soul, and
> with all thy might.
> The gospel says, Herein is love, not that we loved
> God, but that he loved us, and sent his Son to
> be the propitiation for our sins.

> The law says, *Cursed* is every one who continueth
> not in all things written in the book of the law
> to do them.

The gospel says, *Blessed* is the man whose iniquities
are forgiven, and whose sins are covered.

The law says, The *wages* of sin is death.
The gospel says, The *gift* of God is eternal life
through Jesus Christ our Lord.

The law *demands* holiness.
The gospel *gives* holiness.

The law says, *Do.*
The gospel says, *Done.*

The law *extorts* the unwilling service of a bondman.
The gospel *wins* the loving service of a son and
freeman.

The law makes blessings the result of *obedience.*
The gospel makes obedience the result of *blessings.*

The law places the day of rest at the end of the
week's work.
The gospel places it at its beginning.

The law says, *If.*
The gospel says, *Therefore.*

The law was given for the restraint of the old man.
The gospel was given to bring liberty to the
new man.

Under the law, salvation was *wages.*
Under the gospel, salvation is a *gift.*

These two forms of the religious life begin at exactly opposite ends. The religion of legality is as though a man should decide to have an apple orchard and should try to make one by first getting some apples of the kind desired, and then getting a tree and fastening the apples on its branches and then getting roots to fasten to the trunk, and finally purchasing a field in which to plant his manufactured tree. That is, first the fruit, second the branches, third the root, fourth the field. But the religion of grace follows a different order. It begins at the root and grows up and blossoms out into flowers and fruit.

Paul tells us that the law "is our schoolmaster," not our savior; and he emphasizes the fact that it is our schoolmaster only for the purpose of bringing us to Christ, for, after faith in Christ is come, he declares, we are no longer to be under a schoolmaster. He uses the contrast between a servant and a son as an illustration of his meaning. "Wherefore," he says, "thou art no more a servant, but a son"; and he entreats us, because of this, to "stand fast therefore in the liberty where-with Christ hath made us free, and be not entangled again with the yoke of bondage."

It is as if a woman had been a servant in a house, paid for her work in weekly wages, and under the law of her master, whom she had tried to please, but toward whom her service had been one of duty only. Finally, however, the master offers her his love and lifts her up from the place of a servant to be his bride and to share his fortunes. At once the whole spirit of her service is changed. She may perhaps continue to do the same things that she did before, but she does them now altogether from a different motive. The old sense of duty is lost in the new sense of love. The cold word "master" is transformed into the loving word "husband." "And it shall be at that day, saith the LORD, that thou shalt call me Ishi [my husband]; and shalt call me no more Baali [my lord]."

But imagine this bride beginning after a while to look back upon her low estate and to be so overwhelmed by the retrospect as to feel unworthy of union with her husband and to lose consequently the inward sense of this union. Who can doubt that very soon the old sense of working for wages would drive out the new sense of working for love, and in spirit the old name of "my master" would again take the place of the new name of "my husband"?

We exclaim at the folly of such a course. But is not this just what happens to many Christians now? The servitude of duty takes the place of the service of love; and God is looked upon as the stern taskmaster who demands our obedience, instead of the loving Father who wins it.

We all know that nothing so destroys the sweetness of any relation as the creeping in of this legal spirit. The moment a husband and wife cease to perform their services to each other out of a heart of love and union and begin to perform them from a sense of duty alone, that moment the sweetness of the union is lost, and the marriage tie becomes a bondage, and things that were a joy before are turned into crosses. This lies at the bottom, I think, of the current idea of "taking up the cross" in the Christian church. We think it means doing something we ought to do but dislike to do. And such service is thought to be very meritorious toward God, although we all know very well that we would not endure it a moment as toward ourselves. What wife could endure it if her husband should use toward her the language that Christians are continually using toward the Lord; if he should say, for instance, every morning as he went out to the business, "I am going to work for you today, but I wish you to know that it is a very great cross, and I hardly know how to bear it." Or what husband would like such language from his wife? No wonder Paul was alarmed when he found there was danger of a legal spirit such as this creeping into the church of Christ.

Legal Christians do not deny Christ; they only seek to add something to Christ. Their idea is, Christ—and something besides. Perhaps it is Christ and good works, or Christ and earnest feelings, or Christ and clear doctrines, or Christ and certain religious performances. All these are good in themselves and good as the results or fruits of salvation; but to add anything to Christ, no matter how good it may be, as the procuring cause of salvation, is to deny His completeness and to exalt self. Men will undergo many painful self-sacrifices rather than take the place of utter helplessness and worthlessness. A man will gladly be a Saint Simeon Stylites or even a fakir if only it is self that does it so that self may share the glory. And a religion of bondage always exalts self. It is what *I* do—*my* efforts, *my* wrestlings, *my* faithfulness. But a religion of liberty leaves self nothing to glory in; it is all Christ, and what He does, and what He is, and how wonderfully He saves. The child does not boast of himself, but of his father and mother; and our souls can "make their boast in the Lord" when, in this life of liberty, we have learned to know that He and He alone is the sufficient supply for our every need.

We are the children of God and therefore, of course, His heirs; and our possessions come to us, not by working for them, but by inheritance from our Father. Ah, dear friends, how little some of you act like the "heirs of God"! How poverty-stricken you are, and how hard you work for the little you do possess!

You may perhaps point to the results of your legal working or your asceticism, which it is true do seem to have a "show of wisdom in will worship, and humility, and neglecting of the body," as being a proof of the rightness of your course. But I am convinced that whatever really good results there are, have come in spite of, and not because of, your legal working.

I once had a friend whose Christian life was a life of bondage. She worked for her salvation harder than any slave ever worked to purchase his freedom. Among other things, she never felt as if the day could go right for herself or any of her family unless she started it with a long season of wrestling and agonizing and conflict; "winding up her machine," I called it. One day we were talking about it together, and she was telling me of the hardness and bondage of her Christian life and was wondering what the Bible *could* mean when it said Christ's yoke was easy and His burden light. I told her that I thought she must have gotten things wrong somehow, that the Bible always expressed the truth of our relationships with God by using figures that did not admit of any such wrestlings and agonizings as she described. "What would you think," I asked, "of children that had to wrestle and agonize with their parents every morning for their necessary food and clothing or of sheep that had to wrestle with their shepherd before they could secure the necessary care?" "Of course I see that would be all wrong," she said; "but then why do I have such good times after I have gone through these conflicts?" This puzzled me for a moment, but then I asked, "What brings about those good times finally?" "Why, finally," she replied, "I come to the point of trusting the Lord." "Suppose you should come to that point to begin with?" I asked. "Oh," she replied, with a sudden illumination, "I never until this minute thought that I might!"

Christ says that except we "become as little children" we cannot enter into the kingdom of heaven. But it is impossible to get the child-spirit until the servant-spirit has disappeared. Notice, I do not say the spirit of service, but the servant-spirit. Every good child is filled with the spirit of service but ought not to have anything of the servant-spirit. The child serves from love; the servant works for wages.

If a child of loving parents should get the idea that his parents would not give him food and clothing unless he earned them in some way, all the sweetness of the relationship between parent and child would be destroyed. I knew a little girl who did get this idea, and who went around the neighborhood asking at the doors for work, that she might earn a little money to buy herself some clothes. It nearly broke the hearts of her parents when they discovered it. Legal Christians grieve the heart of their heavenly Father, far more than they dream, by letting the servant-spirit creep in, in their relations with Him. As soon as we begin to "work for our living" in spiritual things, we have stepped out of the son's place into the servant's and have "fallen from grace."

One servant of whom we read in the Bible thought his lord was a "hard master"; and the spirit of bondage makes us think the same now. How many Christians there are who have bowed their necks to the yoke of Christ as to a "yoke of bondage," and have read His declaration that His yoke is easy, as though it were a fairy tale, and gone on their way, never dreaming that it was meant to be actually realized as a fact! In truth, so deeply is the idea that the Christian life is a species of bondage ingrained in the church, that, whenever any of the children of God find themselves "walking at liberty" they at once begin to think there must be something wrong in their experience because they no longer find anything to be a "cross" to them. As well might the wife think there must be something wrong in her love for her husband when she finds all her services for him are a pleasure instead of a trial!

Sometimes I think that the whole secret of the Christian life that I have been trying to describe is revealed in the child relationship. Nothing more is needed than just to believe that God is as good a Father as the best ideal earthly father, and that the relationship of a Christian to him is just the same as that of a child to his parents in this world. Children do not need to carry about in their own pockets the money for their support. If the father has plenty, that satisfies them, and is a great deal better than if it were in the child's own possession, since in that case it might get lost. In the same way it is not necessary for Christians to have all their spiritual possessions in their own keeping. It is far better that their riches should be stored up for them in Christ, and that when they want anything they should receive it direct from His hands. He of God is "made unto us wisdom, and righteousness, and sanctification, and redemption"; and apart from Him, we have nothing.

When people are comparative strangers to one another, they cannot with any comfort receive great gifts from each other. But when they are united in spirit, with a bond of true love between them, then, no matter how great the gifts may be that pass from one to the other, they can be accepted without any feeling of embarrassment or obligation on either side.

This principle holds good in the spiritual life. When Christians are living far off from God, they cannot be brought to accept any great gifts from Him. They feel as if they were too unworthy and did not deserve such gifts; and even when He puts the blessing into their very laps, as it were, their false humility prevents them from seeing it, and they go on their way without it.

But when Christians get near enough to the Lord to feel the true spirit of adoption, they are ready to accept with delight all the blessings He has in store for them and never think anything too much to receive. For then they discover that He is only eager, as parents are, to pour out every good gift upon His children, and that, in fact, all things are theirs, because they are Christ's, and Christ is God's.

Sometimes a great mystery is made out of the life hid with Christ in God, as though it were a strange mystical thing that ordinary people could not understand. But this contrast between bondage and liberty makes it very plain. It is only to find out that we really are "no more servants, but sons," and practically to enter into the blessed privileges of this relationship. All can understand what it is to be a little child; there is no mystery about that. God did not use the figure of Father and children without knowing all that this relationship implies; and those, therefore, who know Him as their Father, know the whole secret. They are their Father's heirs and may enter now into possession of all that is necessary for their present needs. They will therefore be very simple in their prayers. "Lord," they will say, "I am your child, and I need such and such things." "My child," He answers, "all things are yours in Christ; come and take just what you need."

Where the executors are honorable men, the heirs to an estate are not obliged to "wrestle" for their inheritance. The executors are appointed, not to keep them out of it, but to help them into possession of it. I sometimes think Christians look upon our Lord as someone appointed to keep them out of their possessions instead of the one who has come to bring them in. They little know how such an implication grieves and dishonors Him.

It is because legal Christians do not know the truth of their relationship to God, as children to a father, and do not recognize His fatherly heart toward them, that they are in bondage. When they do recognize it, the spirit of bondage becomes impossible to them.

Our liberty must come, therefore, from an understanding of the mind and thoughts of God toward us.

What are the facts of the case? If He has called us only

to the servant's place, then the Christians whose lives are lives of weary bondage are right. But if He has called us to be children and heirs, if we are His friends, His brethren, His bride, how sadly and grievously wrong we are in being entangled under any yoke of bondage whatever, no matter how pious a yoke it may seem to be!

The thought of bondage is utterly abhorrent to any of earth's true relationships, and surely it must be more repugnant to heavenly relationship. It will not, of course, hinder the final entrance of the poor enslaved soul into its heavenly rest, but it will, I am sure, put it into the sad condition of those who are described in 1 Corinthians 3:11–15. Their work shall be burned, and they shall suffer loss; yet they themselves shall be saved, but so as by fire.

"Against such there is no law" is the divine sentence concerning all who live and walk in the Spirit; and you shall find it most blessedly true in your own experience if you will but lay aside all self-effort and self-dependence of every kind and will consent to let Christ live in you and work in you and be your indwelling life.

The man who lives by the power of an inward righteous nature is not under bondage to the outward law of righteousness; but he who is restrained by the outward law alone, without the inward restraint of a righteous nature, is a slave to the law. The one fulfills the law in his soul and is therefore free. The other rebels against the law in his soul and is therefore bound.

I would that every child of God did but know the deliverance from bondage which I have tried to set forth!

Let me entreat of you, my readers, to abandon yourselves so utterly to the Lord Jesus Christ that He may be able to "work in you all the good pleasure of His will," and may, by the law of the Spirit of Life in Himself, deliver you from every other law that could possibly enslave you.

Chapter 14

Growth

O ne great objection made against those who advocate this life of faith is that they do not teach a growth in grace. They are supposed to teach that the soul arrives in one moment at a state of perfection, beyond which there is no advance, and that all the exhortations in the scriptures that point toward growth and development are rendered void by this teaching.

Since exactly the opposite of this is true, I will try, if possible, to answer these objections and to show what seems to me the scriptural way of growing and in what place the soul must be in order to grow.

The text which is most frequently quoted is 2 Peter 3:18: "But grow in grace, and in the knowledge of our Lord and Savior Jesus Christ." Now this text expresses exactly what we who teach this life of faith believe to be God's will for us, and what we also believe He has made it possible for us to experience. We accept, in their very fullest meaning, all the commands and promises concerning our being no more children and our growing up into Christ in all things, until we come unto a perfect man, unto the "measure of the stature of the fulness of Christ." We rejoice that we need not continue always to be babes, needing milk; but that we may, by reason of use and development, become such as have need of strong meat, skillful in the word of righteousness and able to discern both good and evil. And none would grieve more than we ourselves at the thought of any finality in the Christian life beyond which there could be no advance.

But then we believe in a growing that does really produce continually progressing maturity and in a development that, as a fact, does bring forth ripe fruit. We expect to reach the aim set before us; and if we do not find ourselves on the way toward it, we feel sure there must be some fault in our growing. No parent would be satisfied with the growth of his child if day after day and year after year, he remained the same helpless babe he was in the first months of his life. And no farmer would feel comfortable under such growing of his grain as should stop short at the blade and never produce the ear or the full corn in the ear. Growth, to be real, must be progressive, and the days and weeks and months should bring a development and increase of maturity in the thing growing. But is this the case with a large part of that which is called growth in grace? Does not the very Christian who is the most strenuous in his longings and his efforts after this growth too often find that, at the end of the year, he is not as far on in his Christian experience as at the beginning, and that his zeal and his devotedness and his separation from the world are not as whole-souled or complete as when his Christian life first began?

I was once urging upon a company of Christians the duty and privilege of an immediate and definite step into the "land of promise," when a lady of great intelligence interrupted me, with what she evidently felt to be a complete rebuttal of all I had been saying, by exclaiming, "Ah! But, Mrs. Smith, I believe in *growing* in grace." "How long have *you* been growing?" I asked. "About twenty-five years," was her answer. "And how much more unworldly and devoted to the Lord are you now than when your Christian life began?" I continued. "Alas!" was the answer. "I fear I am not nearly so much so"; and with this answer, her eyes were opened to see that at all events her way of growing had not been successful but quite the reverse.

The trouble with her, and with every other such case, is simply this: They are trying to grow *into* grace, instead of *in* it. They are like a rosebush, planted by a gardener in the hard, stony path, with a view to its growing *into* the flower bed and which has of course dwindled and withered in consequence, instead of flourishing and maturing. The children of Israel wandering in the wilderness are a perfect picture of this sort of growing. They were traveling about for forty years, taking many weary steps and finding but little rest from their wanderings; and yet, at the end of it all, were no nearer the promised land than they were at the beginning. When they started on their wanderings at Kadesh Barnea, they were at the borders of the land, and a few steps would have taken them into it. When they ended their wanderings in the plains of Moab, they were also at its borders; only with this difference, that now there was a river to cross, which at first there would not have been. All their wanderings and fightings in the wilderness had not put them in possession of one inch of the promised land. In order to get possession of this land, it was necessary first to be in it; and in order to grow in grace, it is necessary first to be planted in grace. When once in the land, however, their conquest was rapid; and when once planted in grace, the growth of the spiritual life becomes vigorous and rapid beyond all conceiving. For grace is a most fruitful soil, and the plants that grow therein are plants of a marvelous growth. They are tended by a divine husbandman and are warmed by the Sun of Righteousness and watered by the dew from heaven. Surely it is no wonder that they bring forth fruit, "some an hundredfold, some sixtyfold, some thirtyfold."

But, it will be asked, what is meant by growing in grace? It is difficult to answer this question because so few people have any conception of what the grace of God really is. To say that it is free unmerited favor only expresses a little of its meaning. It is the unhindered, wondrous, boundless love of God, poured out upon us in an infinite variety of ways, without stint or measure, not according to our deserving but according to His measureless heart of love, which passes knowledge, so unfathomable are its heights and depths. I sometimes think a totally different meaning is given to the word "love" when it is associated with God from that which we so well understand in its human application. We seem to consider that divine love is hard and self-seeking and distant, concerned about its own glory, and indifferent to the fate of others. But if ever human love was tender and self-sacrificing and devoted, if ever it could bear and forbear, if ever it could suffer gladly for its loved one, if ever it was willing to pour itself out in a lavish abandonment for the comfort or pleasure of its objects, then infinitely more is divine love tender and self-sacrificing and devoted, and glad to bear and forbear and suffer, and eager to lavish its best of gifts and blessings upon the objects of its love. Put together all the tenderest love you know of, dear reader, the deepest you have ever felt and the strongest that has ever been poured out upon you, and heap upon it all the love of all the loving human hearts in the world, and then multiply it by infinity, and you will begin perhaps to have some faint glimpses of the love and grace of God!

To "grow in grace," therefore, the soul must be planted in the very heart of this divine love, enveloped by it, steeped in it. It must let itself out to the joy of it and must refuse to know anything else. It must grow in the apprehensions of it, day by day; it must entrust everything to its care and must have no shadow of doubt but that it will surely order all things well.

To grow in grace is opposed to all growth in self-dependence or self-effort—to all legality, in fact, of every kind. It is to put our growing, as well as everything else, into the hands of the Lord and leave it with Him. It is to be so satisfied with our husbandman and with His skill and wisdom, that not a question will cross our minds as to His mode of treatment or His plan of cultivation. It is to grow as the lilies grow, or as the babies grow, without care and without anxiety; to grow by the power of an inward life-principle that cannot help but grow; to grow because we live and therefore must grow; to grow because He who has planted us has planted a growing thing and has made us on purpose to grow.

Surely this is what our Lord meant when He said, "Consider the lilies of the field, how they grow; they toil not, neither do they spin: and yet I say unto you, That even Solomon in all his glory was not arrayed like one of these." Or, when He says again, "Which of you by taking thought can add one cubit unto his stature?" There is no effort in the growing of a babe or of a lily. The lily does not toil nor spin, it does not stretch nor strain, it does not make any effort of any kind to grow, it is not conscious even that it is growing; but by an inward life-principle, and through the nurturing care of God's providence and the fostering of caretaker or gardener, by the heat of the sun and the falling of the rain, it grows and buds and blossoms into the beautiful plant God meant it to be.

The result of this sort of growing in the Christian life is sure. Even Solomon in all his glory, our Lord says, was not arrayed like one of God's lilies. Solomon's array cost much toiling and spinning, and gold and silver in abundance; but the lily's array costs none of these. And though we may toil and spin to make for ourselves beautiful spiritual garments and may strain and stretch in our efforts after spiritual growth, we shall accomplish nothing; for no man by taking thought *can* add one cubit to his stature, and no array of ours can ever equal the beautiful dress with which the great husbandman clothes the plants that grow in His garden of grace and under His fostering care.

Could I but make each one of my readers realize how utterly helpless we are in this matter of growing, I am convinced a large part of the strain would be taken out of many lives at once.

Imagine a child possessed of the monomania that he would not grow unless he made some personal effort after it, and who should insist upon a combination of ropes and pulleys whereby to stretch himself up to the desired height. He might, it is true, spend his days and years in a weary strain, but after all there would be no change in the inexorable fiat, No man "by taking thought can add one cubit unto his stature," and his weary efforts would be only wasted, if they did not actually hinder the longed-for end.

Imagine a lily trying to clothe itself in beautiful colors and graceful lines and drawing to its aid, as so many of God's children try to do, the wisdom and strength of all the lilies around it! I think such a lily would very soon become a chronic "case" of spiritual perplexities and difficulties, similar to some that are familiar to every Christian worker.

Neither child nor lily is ever found doing such a vain and foolish thing as *trying* to grow. But I fear many of God's children are doing exactly this foolish thing. They know that they ought to grow, and they feel within them an instinct that longs for growth; but, instead of letting the divine husbandman care for their growing, as it is surely

His business to do, they think to accomplish it by their own toiling and spinning and stretching and straining; and in consequence they pass their lives in a round of wearisome self-efforts that exhausts their energies, while all the time they find themselves, to their infinite grief, growing backward rather than forward.

> *"Ye flowrets of the field," Siddartha said,*
> *"Who turn your tender faces to the sun,*
> *What secret know ye, that ye grow content?"*

What we all need is to "consider the flowers of the field" and learn their secret. Grow, by all means, dear Christians; but grow, I beseech you, in God's way, which is the only effectual way. See to it that you are planted in grace and then let the divine husbandman cultivate you in His own way and by His own means. Put yourselves out in the sunshine of His presence and let the dew of heaven come down upon you and see what will be the result. Leaves and flowers and fruit must surely come in their season; for your husbandman is skillful, and He never fails in His harvesting. Only see to it that you oppose no hindrance to the shining of the Sun of Righteousness or the falling of the dew from heaven. The thinnest covering may serve to keep off the sunshine and the dew, and the plant may wither, even where these are most abundant. And so also the slightest barrier between your soul and Christ may cause you to dwindle and fade as a plant in a cellar or under a bushel. Keep the sky clear. Open wide every avenue of your being to receive the blessed influences your divine husbandman may bring to bear upon you. Bask in the sunshine of His love. Drink of the waters of His goodness. Keep your face upturned to Him as the flowers do to the sun. Look, and your soul shall live and grow.

But it may be objected here that we are not inanimate flowers but intelligent human beings with personal powers and personal responsibilities. This is true; and it makes this important difference, that what the flower is by nature, we must be by an intelligent and free surrender. To be one of God's lilies means an interior abandonment of the rarest kind. It means that we are to be infinitely passive and yet infinitely active also; passive as regards self and its workings, active as regards attention and response to God. It is very hard to explain this so as to be understood. But it means that we must lay down all the activity of the creature as such and must let only the activities of God work in us and through us and by us. Self must step aside to let God work.

You need make no efforts to grow, therefore; but let your efforts instead be all concentrated on this, that you abide in the Vine. The divine husbandman who has the care of the Vine will care also for you who are His branches and will so prune and purge and water and tend you that you will grow and bring forth fruit, and your fruit shall remain and, like the lily, you shall find yourself arrayed in apparel so glorious that that of Solomon will be as nothing to it.

What if you seem to yourselves to be planted at this moment in a desert soil where nothing can grow! Put yourselves absolutely into the hands of the good husbandman, and He will at once begin to make the very desert blossom as the rose and will cause springs and fountains of water to start up out of its sandy wastes. For the promise is sure that the man who trusts in the Lord "shall be as a tree planted by the waters, and that spreadeth out her roots by the river, and shall not see when heat cometh, but her leaf shall be green; and shall not be careful in the year of drought, neither shall cease from yielding fruit."

It is the great prerogative of our divine husbandman that He is able to turn any soil, whatever it may be like, into the soil of grace the moment we put our growing into His hands. He does not need to transplant us into a different field, but right where we are, with just the circumstances that surround us, He makes His sun to shine and His dew to fall upon us and transforms the very things that were before our greatest hindrances into the chiefest and most blessed means of growth. I care not what the circumstances may be, His wonder-working power can accomplish this; and we must trust Him with it all. Surely He is a husbandman we *can* trust; and if He sends storms or winds or rains or sunshine, all must be accepted at His hands with the most unwavering confidence that He who has undertaken to cultivate us and to bring us to maturity knows the very best way of accomplishing His end and regulates the elements, which are all at His disposal, expressly with a view to our most rapid growth.

Let me entreat of you, then, to give up all your efforts after growing and simply to *let* yourselves grow. Leave it all to the husbandman whose care it is and who alone is able to manage it. No difficulties in your case can baffle Him. If you will only put yourselves absolutely into His hands and let Him have His own way with you, no dwarfing of your growth in the years that are past, no apparent dryness of your inward springs of life, no crookedness or deformity in your development can in the least mar the perfect work that He will accomplish. His own gracious promise to His backsliding children assures you of this. "I will heal their backsliding," He says. "I will love them freely: for mine anger is turned away from him. I will be as the dew unto Israel: he shall grow as the lily, and cast forth his roots as Lebanon. His branches shall spread, and his beauty shall be as the olive tree, and his smell as Lebanon. They that dwell under his shadow shall return; they shall revive as the corn, and grow as the vine: the scent thereof shall be as the wine of Lebanon." And again He says: "Be not afraid. . .for the pastures of the wilderness do spring, for the tree beareth her fruit, the fig tree and the vine do yield their strength. . . . And the floors shall be full of wheat, and the vats shall overflow with wine and oil. And I will restore to you the years that the locust hath eaten. . . . And ye shall eat in plenty, and be satisfied, and praise the name of the LORD your God, that hath dealt wondrously with you: and my people shall never be ashamed."

Oh, that you could but know just what your Lord meant when He said, "Consider the lilies of the field, *how they grow; they toil not, neither do they spin*"! Surely these words give us the picture of a life and growth far different from the ordinary life and growth of Christians—a life of rest and a growth without effort; and yet a life and a growth crowned with glorious results. And to every soul that will thus become a lily in the garden of the Lord and will grow as the lilies grow, the same glorious array will be as surely given as was given to them; and they will know the fulfillment of that wonderful mystical passage concerning their Beloved, that "He feedeth among the lilies."

> *I feel as weak as a violet*
> *Alone with the awful sky:*
> *Winds wander, and dews drop earthward,*
> *Rains fall, suns rise and set,*
> *Earth whirls; and all but to prosper*
> *A poor little violet!*

We may rest assured of this, that all the resources of God's infinite grace will be brought to bear on the growing of the tiniest flower in His spiritual garden as certainly as they are in His earthly creation; and as the violet abides peacefully in its little place, content to receive its daily portion without concerning itself about the wandering of the winds or the falling of the rain, so must we repose in the present moment as it comes to us from God, contented with our daily portion and without anxious thought as to anything that may be whirling around us in God's glorious universe, sure that all things will be made to "prosper" for us.

This is the kind of "growth in grace" in which we who have entered into the life of full trust, believe; a growth without care or anxiety on our part, but a growth which does actually grow, which blossoms out into flower and fruit and becomes like a "tree planted by the rivers of water, that bringeth forth his fruit in his season"; whose leaf also does not wither, and who prospers in whatsoever he doeth. And we rejoice to know that there are growing up now in the Lord's heritage many such plants, who, as the lilies behold the face of the sun and grow thereby, are, by "beholding as in a glass the glory of the Lord," being changed into the same image from glory to glory, even as by the Spirit of the Lord.

Should you ask such how it is that they grow so rapidly and with such success, their answer would be that they are not concerned about their growing and are hardly conscious that they do grow. That their Lord has told them to abide in Him and has promised that, if they do thus abide, they shall certainly bring forth much fruit; and that they are concerned, therefore, only about the abiding, which is their part, and are content to leave the cultivating and the growing and the training and the pruning to their good husbandman, who alone is able to manage those things or to bring them about. You will find that such souls are not engaged in watching self, but in "looking unto Jesus." They do not "toil and spin" for their spiritual garments but leave themselves in the hands of the Lord to be arrayed as it may please Him. Self-effort and self-dependence are at an end with them. Formerly they tried to be not only the garden but the gardener as well and undertook to fulfill the duties of both. Now they are content to *be* what they *are*—the garden only, and not the gardener; and they are willing to leave the gardener's duties to the divine husbandman, who alone is responsible for their rightful performance. Their interest in self is gone, transferred over into the hands of another; and self, in consequence, has become nothing to them more and more, and Christ alone is seen to be all in all. And the blessed result is that not even Solomon, in all his glory, was arrayed as these shall be.

Let us look at the subject practically. We all know that growing is not a thing of effort but is the result of an inward life-principle of growth. All the stretching and pulling in the world could not make a dead oak grow; but a live oak grows without stretching. It is plain, therefore, that the essential thing is to get within you the growing life and then you cannot help but grow. And this life is the "life hid with Christ in God," the wonderful divine life of an indwelling Holy Spirit. Be filled with this, dear believer and, whether you are conscious of it or not, you must grow; you cannot help growing. Do not trouble about your growing, but see to it that you have the growing life. Abide in the Vine. Let the life from Him flow through all your spiritual veins. Interpose no barrier to His mighty life-giving power, "working in you all the good pleasure of His will." Yield yourself up utterly to His lovely control. Put your growing into His hands as completely as you have put all your other affairs. Suffer Him to manage it as He will. Do not concern yourself about it, nor even think of it. Do not, as children do, keep digging up your plants to see if they are growing. Trust the divine husbandman absolutely and always. Accept each moment's dispensation as it comes to you, from His dear hands, as being the needed sunshine or dew for that moment's growth. Say a continual "Yes" to your Father's will.

And finally, in this, as in all the other cares of your life, "Be careful for nothing; but in every thing by prayer and supplication with thanksgiving let your requests be made known unto God. And the peace of God, which passeth all understanding, shall keep your hearts and minds through Christ Jesus."

If your "growth in grace" is of this sort, dear reader, you will surely know, sooner or later, a wonderful growing, and you will come to understand, as you cannot now, it may be, what the psalmist meant when he said, "The righteous shall flourish like the palm tree: he shall grow like a cedar in Lebanon. Those that be planted in the house of the LORD shall flourish in the courts of our God. They shall bring forth fruit in old age; they shall be fat and flourishing."

Chapter 15

Service

There is, perhaps, no part of Christian experience where a greater change is known upon entering into this life hid with Christ in God than in the matter of service.

In all the ordinary forms of Christian life, service is apt to have more or less of bondage in it; that is, it is done purely as a matter of duty and often as a trial and a cross. Certain things, which at the first may have been a joy and a delight, become after a while weary tasks, performed faithfully, perhaps, but with much secret disinclination and many confessed or unconfessed wishes that they need not be done at all, or at least that they need not be done so often. The soul finds itself saying, instead of the "May I?" of love, the "Must I?" of duty. The yoke, which was at first easy, begins to gall, and the burden feels heavy instead of light.

One dear Christian expressed it once to me in this way: "When I was first converted," she said, "I was so full of joy and love, that I was only too glad and thankful to be allowed to do anything for my Lord, and I eagerly entered every open door. But after a while, as my early joy faded away, and my love burned less fervently, I began to wish I had not been quite so eager; for I found myself involved in lines of service that were gradually becoming very distasteful and burdensome to me. Since I had begun them, I could not very well give them up without exciting great remark, and yet I longed to do so increasingly. I was expected to visit the sick and pray beside their beds. I was expected to attend prayer meetings and speak at them. I was expected, in short, to be always ready for every effort in Christian work, and the sense of these expectations bowed me down continually. At last it became so unspeakably burdensome to me to live the sort of Christian life I had entered upon and was expected by all around me to live, that I felt as if any kind of manual labor would have been easier; and I would have infinitely preferred scrubbing all day on my hands and knees to being compelled to go through the treadmill of my daily Christian work. I envied," she said, "the servants in the kitchen, and the women at the wash-tubs."

This may seem to some like a strong statement; but does it not present a vivid picture of some of your own experiences, dear Christian? Have you never gone to your work as a slave to his daily task, believing it to be your duty and that, therefore, you must do it, but rebounding like an India-rubber ball back into your real interests and pleasures the moment your work was over?

You have known of course that this was the wrong way to feel and have been thoroughly ashamed of it, but still you have seen no way to help it. You have not *loved* your work; and, could you have done so with an easy conscience, you would have been glad to give it up altogether.

Or, if this does not describe your case, perhaps another picture will. You do love your work in the abstract, but in the doing of it you find so many cares and responsibilities connected with it and feel so many misgivings and doubts as to your own capacity or fitness that it becomes a very heavy burden, and you go to it bowed down and weary before the labor has even begun. Then also you are continually distressing yourself about the results of your work and greatly troubled if they are not just what you would like; and this of itself is a constant burden.

Now, from all these forms of bondage the soul that enters fully into the blessed life of faith is entirely delivered. In the first place, service of any sort becomes delightful to it because, having surrendered its will into the keeping of the Lord, He works in it to will and to do of His good pleasure, and the soul finds itself really *wanting* to do the things God wants it to do. It is always very pleasant to do the things we *want* to do, let them be ever so difficult of accomplishment or involve ever so much of bodily weariness. If a man's *will* is really set on a thing, he regards with a sublime indifference the obstacles that lie in the way of his reaching it and laughs to himself at the idea of any opposition or difficulties hindering him. How many men have gone gladly and thankfully to the ends of the world in search of worldly fortunes or to fulfill worldly ambitions and have scorned the thought of any "cross" connected with it! How many mothers have congratulated themselves and rejoiced over the honor done their sons in seeing them promoted to some place of power and usefulness in their country's service, although it has involved perhaps years of separation and a life of hardship for their dear ones! And yet these same men, and these very mothers, would have felt and said that they were taking up crosses too heavy almost to be borne had the service of Christ required the same sacrifice of home and friends and worldly ease.

It is altogether the way we look at things, whether we think they are crosses or not. And I am ashamed to think that any Christian should ever put on a long face and shed tears over doing a thing for Christ, which a worldly man would be only too glad to do for money.

What we need in the Christian life is to get believers to *want* to do God's will as much as other people want to do their own will. And this is the idea of the gospel. It is what God intended for us; and it is what He has promised. In describing the new covenant in Hebrews 8:6–13, He says it shall no more be the old covenant made on Sinai—that is, a law given from the outside, controlling a man by force—but it shall be a law written *within,* constraining a man by love. "I will put my laws," He says, "into their mind, and write them in their hearts." This can mean nothing but that we shall *love* His law; for anything written in our hearts we must love. "And putting it into our mind" is surely the same as God working in us to "will and to do of His good pleasure," and means that we shall will what God wills and shall obey His sweet commands, not because it is our duty to do so, but because we ourselves want to do what He wants us to do.

Nothing could possibly be conceived more effectual than this. How often have we thought, when dealing with our children, "Oh, if I could only get inside of them and make them *want* to do just what I want, how easy it would be to manage them then!" How often in practical experience we have found that, to deal with cross-grained people, we most carefully avoid suggesting our wishes to them but must in some way induce them to suggest the thing themselves, sure that there will then be no opposition to contend with. And we, who are by nature a stiff-necked people, always rebel more or less against a law from outside of us while we joyfully embrace the same law springing up within.

God's way of working, therefore, is to get possession of the inside of a man, to take the control and management of his will, and to work it for him. Then obedience is easy and a delight, and service becomes perfect freedom; until the Christian is forced to exclaim, "This happy service! Who could dream earth had such liberty?"

What you need to do then, dear Christian, if you are in bondage in the matter of service, is to put your will over completely into the hands of your Lord, surrendering to Him the entire control of it. Say, "Yes, Lord, *yes!*" to everything, and trust Him so to work in you to will, as to bring your whole wishes and affections into conformity with His own sweet and lovable and most lovely will. I have seen this done often in cases where it looked beforehand an utterly impossible thing. In one case, where a lady had been for years rebelling fearfully against a little act of service which she knew was right, but which she hated, I saw her, out of the depths of despair, and without any feeling whatever, give her will in that matter up into the hands of her Lord and begin to say to Him, "Thy will be done; *Thy will be done!*" And in one short hour, that very thing began to look sweet and precious to her.

It is wonderful what miracles God works in wills that are utterly surrendered to Him. He turns hard things into easy, and bitter things into sweet. It is not that He puts easy things in the place of the hard, but He actually changes the hard thing into an easy one and makes us love to do the thing we before so hated. While we rebel against the yoke and try to avoid it, we find it hard and galling. But when we "take the yoke upon us" with a consenting will, we find it easy and comfortable. It is said of Ephraim that at one time he was like "a bullock unaccustomed to the yoke," but that afterwards, when he had submitted to the yoke, he was "as an heifer that is taught, and *loveth* to tread out the corn."

Many Christians, as I have said, love God's will in the abstract but carry great burdens in connection with it. From this also there is deliverance in the wonderful life of faith. For in this life no burdens are carried, no anxieties felt. The Lord is our burden-bearer, and upon Him we must lay off every care. He says, in effect, "Be careful for nothing, but make your requests known to Me, and I will attend to them all." Be careful for *nothing,* He says, not even your service. Above all, I should think, our service, because we know ourselves to be so utterly helpless in regard to it, that, even if we were careful, it would not amount to anything. What have we to do with thinking whether we are fit or not? The Master-workman surely has a right to use any tool He pleases for His own work, and it is plainly not the business of the tool to decide whether it is the right one to be used or not. He knows, and if He chooses to use us, of course we must be fit. And in truth, if we only knew it, our chief fitness is in our utter helplessness. His strength is made perfect, not in our strength, but in our weakness. Our strength is only a hindrance.

I was once visiting an insane asylum and saw the children going through dumbbell exercises. Now we all know that it is sometimes difficult for the mentally ill to manage their movements. They have strength enough, generally, but no skill to use this strength, and as a consequence cannot do much. And, in these dumbbell exercises, this deficiency was very apparent. They made all sorts of awkward movements. Now and then, by a happy chance, they would make a movement in harmony with the music and the teacher's directions, but for the most part all was out of harmony. One little girl, however, I noticed made perfect movements. Not a jar or a break disturbed the harmony of her exercises. And the reason was, not that she had more strength than the others, but that she had no strength at all. She could not so much as close her hands over the dumbbells, nor lift her arms, and the master had to stand behind her and do it all. She yielded up her members as instruments to him, and his "strength was made perfect" in her weakness. He knew how to go through those exercises, for he himself had planned them; and therefore, when he did it, it was done right. She did nothing but yield herself up utterly into his hands, and he did it all. The yielding was her part; the responsibility was all his. It was not her skill that was needed to make harmonious movements, but only his. The question was not of her capacity, but of his. Her utter weakness was her greatest strength.

To me this is a very striking picture of our Christian life, and it is no wonder, therefore, that Paul could say, "Most gladly therefore will I rather *glory* in my infirmities, that the power of Christ may rest upon me." Who would not glory in being so utterly weak and helpless that the Lord Jesus Christ should find no hindrance to the perfect working of His mighty power through us and in us?

Then, too, if the work is His, the responsibility is His also, and we have no room left for worrying about results. Everything in reference to it is known to Him, and He can manage it all. Why not leave it all with Him, then, and consent to be "treated like a child and guided where to go"? It is a fact that the most effectual workers I know are those who do not feel the least care or anxiety about their work, but who commit it all to their dear Master, and, asking Him to guide them moment by moment in reference to it, trust Him implicitly for each moment's needed supplies of wisdom and of strength. To look at them, you would almost think perhaps that they were too free from care, where such mighty interests are at stake. But when you have learned God's secret of trusting and see the beauty and the power of the life that is yielded up to His working, you will cease to condemn and will begin to wonder how any of God's workers can dare carry the burdens or assume the responsibilities which He alone is able to bear.

Some may object that the Apostle Paul spoke of the "care of the churches" coming upon him. But we must not fail to remember that it was the constant habit of the apostle to roll every care off on the Lord, and thus, while full of care, to be "without carefulness."

There are one or two other bonds in service from which this life of trust delivers us. We find out that no one individual is responsible for all the work in the world, but only for a small share. Our duty ceases to be universal and becomes personal and individual. The Master does not say to us "Go and do everything," but He marks out a special path for each of us and gives to each one of us a special duty. There are "diversities of gifts" in the kingdom of God, and these gifts are divided to "every man according to his several ability." I may have five talents, or two, or only one; I may be called to do twenty things or only one. My responsibility is simply to do that which I am called to do and nothing more. "The *steps* of a good man are ordered by the LORD"; not his way only, but each separate step in that way.

Many Christians make the further mistake of looking upon every act of service as a perpetual obligation. They think because it was right for them to give a tract to one person in a railway train, for instance, that, therefore, they are always to give tracts to everybody, and in this way they burden themselves with an impossible duty.

There was a young Christian once who, because she had been sent to speak a message to one soul whom she met in a walk, supposed it was a perpetual obligation and thought she must speak about their souls to every one she met in her walks. This was of course impossible, and as a consequence she was soon in hopeless bondage about it. She became absolutely afraid to go outside of her own door and lived in perpetual condemnation. At last she disclosed her distress to a friend who was instructed in the ways of God with His servants; and this friend told her she was making a great mistake; that the Lord had His own special work for each special workman, and that the servants in a well-regulated household might as well each one take it upon themselves to try to do the work of all the rest as for the Lord's servants to think they were each one under obligation to do everything. He told her just to put herself under the Lord's personal guidance as to her work and trust Him to point out to her each particular person to whom He would have her speak, assuring her that He never puts forth His own sheep without going before them and making a way for them Himself. She followed this advice and laid the burden of her work on the Lord, and the result was a happy pathway of daily guidance in which she was led into much blessed work for her master and was able to do it all without a care or a burden because He led her out and prepared the way before her.

I have been very much instructed myself by thinking of the arrangements of our own households. When we appoint a servant for a special part of the work of the household, we want him to attend to that alone and not run all over the house trying to attend to the work of all the other servants. It would make endless confusion in any earthly household if the servants were to act in this fashion, and it makes no less confusion in the divine household.

Our part in the matter of service seems to me just like making the junction between the machinery and the steam-engine. The power is not in the machinery but in the steam. Disconnected from the engine, the machinery is perfectly useless. But let the connection be made, and the machinery goes easily and without effort because of the mighty power there is behind it. Thus the Christian life, when it is the development of the divine life working within, becomes an easy and natural life. Most Christians live on a strain because their wills are not fully in harmony with the will of God, the connection is not perfectly made at every point, and it requires an effort to move the machinery. But when once the connection is fully made and the "law of the Spirit of life in Christ Jesus" can work in us with all its mighty power, we are then indeed made "free from the law of sin and death," and shall know the glorious liberty of the children of God.

Another form of bondage as to service, from which the life of faith delivers the soul, is in reference to the after-reflections which always follow any Christian work. These after-reflections are of two sorts: either the soul congratulates itself upon its success and is lifted up; or it is distressed over its failure and is utterly cast down. One of these is *sure* to come; and of the two I think the former is the more to be dreaded, although the latter causes at the time the greater suffering. But in the life of trust neither will trouble us; for, having committed ourselves in our work to the Lord, we shall be satisfied to leave it to Him and shall not think about ourselves in the matter at all.

Years ago I came across this sentence in an old book: "Never indulge, at the close of an action, in any self-reflective acts of any kind, whether of self-congratulation or of self-despair. Forget the things that are behind the moment they are past, leaving them with God." This has been of unspeakable value to me. When the temptation comes, as it mostly does to every worker after the performance of any service, to indulge in these reflections, either of one sort or the other, I turn from them at once and positively refuse to think about my work at all, leaving it with the Lord to overrule the mistakes and to bless it as He chooses. I believe there would be far fewer "blue Mondays" for ministers of the gospel than there are now if they would adopt this plan; and I am sure all workers would find their work far less wearing.

To sum it all up, then, what is needed for happy and effectual service is simply to put your work into the Lord's hands and leave it there. Do not take it to Him in prayer, saying, "Lord, guide me; Lord, give me wisdom; Lord, arrange for me," and then rise from your knees and take the burden all back and try to guide and arrange for yourself. *Leave* it with the Lord; and remember that what you trust to Him, you must not worry over nor feel anxious about. Trust and worry cannot go together. If your work is a burden, it is because you are not trusting it to Him. But if you do trust it to Him, you will surely find that the yoke He puts upon you is easy, and the burden He gives you to carry is light; and, even in the midst of a life of ceaseless activity, you shall "find rest to your soul."

If the divine Master only had a band of such workers as this, there is no limit to what He might do with them. Truly, one such would "chase a thousand, and two would put ten thousand to flight," and nothing would be impossible to them. For it is nothing with the Lord "to help, whether with many, or with them that have no power," if only He can find instruments that are fully abandoned to His working.

May God raise up such an army speedily! And may you, my dear reader, enroll your name among this band and, yielding yourself unto God as one who is "alive from the dead," may every one of your members be also yielded unto Him as "instruments of righteousness," to be used by Him as He pleases!

Chapter 16

Practical Results in the Daily Walk and Conversation

If all that has been written in the foregoing chapters on the life hid with Christ be true, its results in the practical daily walk and conversation ought to be very marked, and the people who have entered into the enjoyment of it ought to be, in very truth, a peculiar people, zealous of good works.

My son, now with God, once wrote to a friend something to this effect: that we are God's witnesses necessarily, because the world will not read the Bible, but they will read our lives; and that upon the report these give will very much depend their belief in the divine nature of the religion we possess. This age is essentially an age of facts, and all scientific inquiries are being increasingly turned from theories to realities. If, therefore, our religion is to make any headway in the present time, it must be proved to be more than a theory; and we must present to the investigation of the critical minds of our age the realities of lives transformed by the mighty power of God, "working in them all the good pleasure of His will."

I desire, therefore, to speak very solemnly for what I conceive to be the necessary fruits of a life of faith such as I have been describing and to press home to the hearts of every one of my readers their personal responsibility to "walk worthy of the high calling" wherewith they have been called.

I think that I may speak to some of you, at least, as personal friends, for I feel sure we have not gone thus far together through these pages, without there having grown in your hearts, as there has in mine, a tender personal interest and longing for one another, that we may in everything show forth the praises of Him who has "called us out of darkness into his marvellous light." As a friend, then, to friends, I speak, and I am sure I shall be pardoned if I go into some details of our daily lives, which may seem of secondary importance and which make up the largest part of them.

The standard of practical holy living has been so low among Christians that the least degree of real devotedness of life and walk is looked upon with surprise and often even with disapprobation by a large portion of the church. And, for the most part, the followers of the Lord Jesus Christ are satisfied with a life so conformed to the world and so like it in almost every respect, that, to a casual observer, no difference is discernible.

But we, who have heard the call of our God to a life of entire consecration and perfect trust, must do differently. We must come out from the world and be separate and must not be conformed to it in our characters or in our lives. We must set our affections on heavenly things, not on earthly ones, and must seek first the kingdom of God and His righteousness; surrendering every thing that would interfere with this. We must walk through the world as Christ walked. We must have the mind that was in Him. As pilgrims and strangers, we must abstain from fleshly lusts that war against the soul. As good soldiers of Jesus Christ, we must disentangle ourselves inwardly from the affairs of this life that we may please Him who has chosen us to be soldiers. We must abstain from all appearance of evil. We must be kind to one another, tender-hearted, forgiving one another, even as God, for Christ's sake, has forgiven us. We must not resent injuries or unkindness but must return good for evil and turn the other cheek to the hand that smites us. We must take always the lowest place among our fellowmen and seek not our own honor, but the honor of others. We must be gentle and meek and yielding; not standing up for our own rights, but for the rights of others. We must do everything, not for our own glory, but for the glory of God. And, to sum it all up, since He who has called us is holy, so we must be holy in all manner of conversation; because it is written, "Be ye holy, for I am holy."

Some Christians seem to think that all the requirements of a holy life are met when there is very active and successful Christian work; and because they do so much for the Lord in public, they feel a liberty to be cross and ugly and un-Christlike in private. But this is not the sort of Christian life I am depicting. If we are to walk as Christ walked, it must be in private as well as in public, at home as well as abroad; and it must be every hour all day long and not at stated periods or on certain fixed occasions. We must be just as Christlike to our servants as we are to our minister and just as "good" in our counting house as we are in our prayer meeting.

It is in daily homely living, indeed, that practical piety can best show itself, and we may well question any "professions" that fail under this test of daily life.

A cross Christian, or an anxious Christian, a discouraged, gloomy Christian, a doubting Christian, a complaining Christian, an exacting Christian, a selfish Christian, a cruel, hard-hearted Christian, a self-indulgent Christian, a Christian with a sharp tongue or bitter spirit, all these may be very earnest in their work and may have honorable places in the church; but they are *not* Christlike Christians, and they know nothing of the realities of which this book treats, no matter how loud their professions may be.

The life hid with Christ in God is a hidden life, as to its source, but it must not be hidden as to its practical results. People must see that we walk as Christ walked if we say that we are abiding in Him. We must prove that we "possess" that which we "profess." We must, in short, be real followers of Christ and not theoretical ones only. And this means a great deal. It means that we must really and absolutely turn our backs on everything that is contrary to the perfect will of God. It means that we are to be a "peculiar people," not only in the eyes of God but in the eyes of the world around us; and that, wherever we go, it will be known from our habits, our tempers, our conversation, and our pursuits, that we are followers of the Lord Jesus Christ and are not of the world, even as He was not of the world. We must no longer look upon our money as our own, but as belonging to the Lord, to be used in His service. We must not feel at liberty to use our energies exclusively in the pursuit of worldly means but must recognize, that, if we seek first the kingdom of God and His righteousness, all needful things shall be added unto us. We shall find ourselves forbidden to seek the highest places or to strain after worldly advantages. We shall not be permitted to make self, as heretofore, the center of all our thoughts and all our aims. Our days will have to be spent not in serving ourselves but in serving the Lord; and we shall find ourselves called upon to bear one another's burdens and so fulfill the law of Christ. And all our daily homely duties will be more perfectly performed than ever because whatever we do will be done, "not with eyeservice, as menpleasers; but as the servants of Christ, doing the will of God from the heart."

Into all this we shall undoubtedly be led by the Spirit of God if we give ourselves up to His guidance. But unless we have the right standard of Christian life set before us, we may be hindered by our ignorance from recognizing His voice; and it is for this reason I desire to be very plain and definite in my statements.

I have noticed that wherever there has been a faithful following of the Lord in a consecrated soul, several things have, sooner or later, inevitably followed.

Meekness and quietness of spirit become in time the characteristics of the daily life. A submissive acceptance of the will of God, as it comes in the hourly events of each day, is manifested; pliability in the hands of God to do or to suffer all the good pleasure of His will; sweetness under provocation; calmness in the midst of turmoil and bustle; a yielding to the wishes of others, and an insensibility to slights and affronts; absence of worry or anxiety; deliverance from care and fear—all these, and many other similar graces, are invariably found to be the natural outward development of that inward life which is hid with Christ in God. Then as to the habits of life: We always see such Christians sooner or later laying aside thoughts of self and becoming full of consideration for others; they dress and live in simple, healthful ways; they renounce self-indulgent habits and surrender all purely fleshly gratifications. Some helpful work for others is taken up and useless occupations are dropped out of the life. God's glory, and the welfare of His creatures, become the absorbing delight of the soul. The voice is dedicated to Him to be used in singing His praises. The purse is placed at His disposal. The pen is dedicated to write for Him, the lips to speak for Him, the hands and the feet to do His bidding. Year after year such Christians are seen to grow more unworldly, more serene, more heavenly minded, more transformed, more like Christ until even their very faces express so much of the beautiful inward divine life that all who look at them cannot but take knowledge of them that they live with Jesus and are abiding in Him.

I feel sure that to each one of you have come some divine intimations or foreshadowings of the life I here describe. Have you not begun to feel dimly conscious of the voice of God speaking to you, in the depths of your soul, about these things? Has it not been a pain and a distress to you of late to discover how full your lives are of self? Has not your soul been plunged into inward trouble and doubt about certain dispositions or pursuits in which you have been formerly accustomed to indulge? Have you not begun to feel uneasy with some of your habits of life and to wish that you could do differently in certain respects? Have not paths of devotedness and of service begun to open out before you with the longing thought, "Oh, that I could walk them!" All these questions and doubts and this inward yearning are the voice of the good shepherd in your heart, seeking to call you out of that which is contrary to His will. Let me entreat of you not to turn away from His gentle pleadings! You little know the sweet paths into which He means to lead you by these very steps, nor the wonderful stores of blessedness that lie at their end, or you would spring forward with an eager joy to yield to every one of His requirements. The heights of Christian perfection can only be reached by each moment faithfully following the guide who is to lead you there; and He reveals the way to us one step at a time, in the little things of our daily lives, asking only on our part that we yield ourselves up to His guidance. Be perfectly pliable then in His dear hands to go where He entices you and to turn away from all from which He makes you shrink. Obey Him perfectly the moment you are sure of His will; and you will soon find that He is leading you out swiftly and easily into such a wonderful life of conformity to Himself that it will be a testimony to all around you, beyond what you yourself will ever know.

I knew a soul thus given up to follow the Lord whithersoever He might lead her, who in a very little while traveled from the depths of darkness and despair into the realization and actual experience of a most blessed union with the Lord Jesus Christ. Out of the midst of her darkness she consecrated herself to the Lord, surrendering her will up altogether to Him, that He might work in her to will and to do of His own good pleasure. Immediately He began to speak to her by His Spirit in her heart, suggesting to her some little acts of service for Him and troubling her about certain things in her habits and her life, showing her where she was selfish and un-Christlike and how she could be transformed. She recognized His voice and yielded to Him each thing He asked for, the moment she was sure of His will. Her swift obedience was rewarded by a rapid progress, and day by day she was conformed more and more to the image of Christ until very soon her life became such a testimony to those around her that some even who had begun by opposing and disbelieving were forced to acknowledge that it was of God and were won to a similar surrender. And finally, in a little while it came to pass, so swiftly had she gone, that her Lord was able to reveal to her wondering soul some of the deepest secrets of His love and to fulfill to her the marvelous promise of Acts 1:5, by giving her to realize the baptism of the Holy Ghost. Think you she has ever regretted her whole-hearted following of Him? Or that aught but thankfulness and joy can ever fill her soul when she reviews the steps by which her feet have been led to this place of wondrous blessedness, even though some of them may have seemed at the time hard to take? Ah, dear soul, if you would know a like blessing, abandon yourself, like her, to the guidance of your divine master and shrink from no surrender for which He may call.

The perfect way is hard to flesh,
It is not hard to love;
If thou wert sick for want of God,
How swiftly wouldst thou move!

Surely you can trust Him! And if some things may be called for that look to you of but little moment and not worthy of your Lord's attention, remember that He sees not as man sees, and that things small to you may be in His eyes the key and the clue to the deepest springs of your being. No life can be complete that fails in its little things. A look, a word, a tone of voice even, however small they may seem to human judgment, are often of vital importance in the eyes of God. Your one great desire is to follow Him fully; can you not say then a continual "Yes" to all His sweet commands, whether small or great, and trust Him to lead you, by the shortest road, to your fullest blessedness?

My dear friend, whether you knew it or not, this, and nothing less than this, is what your consecration meant. It meant inevitable obedience. It meant that the will of your God was henceforth to be your will, under all circumstances and at all times. It meant that from that moment you did surrender your liberty of choice and gave yourself up utterly into the control of your Lord. It meant an hourly following of Him, whithersoever He might lead you, without any turning back.

All this and far more was involved in your surrender to God, and now I appeal to you to make good your word. Let everything else go that you mayst live out, in a practical daily walk and conversation, the Christ-life you have dwelling within you. You are united to your Lord by a wondrous tie; walk, then, as He walked and show to the unbelieving world the blessed reality of His mighty power to save by letting Him save you to the very uttermost. You need not fear to consent to this for He is your Savior, and His power is to do it all. He is not asking you, in your poor weakness, to do it yourself; He only asks you to yield yourself to Him that He may work in you and through you by His own mighty power. Your part is to yield yourself; His part is to work; and never, never will He give you any command that is not accompanied by ample power to obey it. Take no thought for the morrow in this matter; but abandon yourself with a generous trust to the good Shepherd, who has promised never to call His own sheep out into any path without Himself going before them to make the way easy and safe. Take each little step as He makes it plain to you. Bring all your life, in each of its details, to Him to regulate and guide. Follow gladly and quickly the sweet suggestions of His Spirit in your soul. And day by day you will find Him bringing you more and more into conformity with His will in all things; molding you and fashioning you, as you are able to bear it, into a "vessel unto His honor, sanctified and meet for His use, and fitted to every good work." So shall be given to you the sweet joy of being an "epistle of Christ, known and read of all men"; and your light shall shine so brightly, that men seeing not you but your good works shall glorify not you but your Father which is in heaven.

> But thou art making me, I thank thee, Sire.
> What thou hast done and doest, thou knowest well,
> And I will help thee: gently in thy fire
> I will lie burning; on thy potter's wheel
> I will whirl patient, though my brain should reel;
> Thy grace shall be enough the grief to quell,
> And growing strength perfect, through weakness dire.
> I have not knowledge, wisdom, insight, thought,
> Nor understanding, fit to justify

Thee to thy work, O Perfect! Thou hast brought
Me up to this; and lo! What thou hast wrought,
I cannot comprehend. But I can cry,
"O enemy, the Maker hath not done;
One day thou shalt behold, and from the sight shalt
run!"

Thou workest perfectly. And if it seem
Some things are not so well, 'tis but because
They are too loving deep, too lofty wise,
For me, poor child, to understand their laws.
My highest wisdom, half is but a dream;
My love runs helpless like a falling stream;
Thy good embraces ill, and lo! its illness dies.

—George MacDonald

Chapter 17

The Joy of Obedience

Having spoken of some of the difficulties in this life of faith, let me now speak of some of its joys. And foremost among these stands the joy of obedience.

Long ago I met somewhere with this sentence, "Perfect obedience would be perfect happiness, if only we had perfect confidence in the power we were obeying." I remember being struck with the saying as the revelation of a possible, although hitherto undreamed of, way of happiness; and often afterwards, even when full of inward rebellion, did that saying recur to me as the vision of a rest, and yet of a possible development, that would soothe and at the same time satisfy all my yearnings.

Need I say that this rest has been revealed to me now, not as a vision, but as a reality; and that I have seen in the Lord Jesus the master to whom we may yield up our implicit obedience and, taking His yoke upon us, may find our perfect rest?

You little know, dear hesitating soul, of the joy you are missing. The master has revealed Himself to you and is calling for your complete surrender, and you shrink and hesitate. A measure of surrender you are willing to make and think indeed it is fit and proper that you should. But an *utter* abandonment, without any reserves, seems to you too much to be asked for. You are afraid of it. It involves too much, you think, and is too great a risk. To be measurably obedient you desire; to be perfectly obedient appalls you.

Then, too, you see other souls who seem able to walk with easy consciences in a far wider path than that which appears to be marked out for you, and you ask yourself why this need be. It seems strange, and perhaps hard to you, that you must do what they need not and must leave undone what they have liberty to do.

Ah! Dear Christian, this very difference between you is your privilege, though you do not yet know it. Your Lord says, "He that *hath* my commandments, and keepeth them, he it is that loveth me: and he that loveth me shall be loved of my Father, and I will love him, and will manifest myself to him." You *have* His commandments; those you envy have them not. *You* know the mind of your Lord about many things, in which, as yet, *they* are walking in darkness. Is not this a privilege? Is it a cause for regret that your soul is brought into such near and intimate relations with your master that He is able to tell you things which those who are farther off may not know? Do you not realize what a tender degree of intimacy is implied in this?

There are many relations in life that require from the different parties only very moderate degrees of devotion. We may have really pleasant friendships with one another and yet spend a large part of our lives in separate interests and widely differing pursuits. When together, we may greatly enjoy one another's society and find many congenial points; but separation is not any especial distress to us, and other and more intimate friendships do not interfere. There is not enough love between us to give us either the right or the desire to enter into and share one another's most private affairs. A certain degree of reserve and distance seems to be the suitable thing in such relations as these. But there are other relations in life where all this is changed. The friendship becomes love. The two hearts give themselves to each other, to be no longer two, but one. A union of soul takes place, which makes all that belongs to one the property of the other. Separate interests and separate paths in life are no longer possible. Things that were lawful before become unlawful now because of the nearness of the tie that binds. The reserve and distance suitable to mere friendship become fatal in love. Love gives all and must have all in return. The wishes of one become binding obligations to the other, and the deepest desire of each heart is that it may know every secret wish or longing of the other in order that it may fly on the wings of the wind to gratify it.

Do such as these chafe under this yoke which love imposes? Do they envy the cool, calm, reasonable friendships they see around them and regret the nearness into which their souls are brought to their beloved one because of the obligations it creates? Do they not rather glory in these very obligations and inwardly pity, with a tender yet exulting joy, the poor far-off ones who dare not come so near? Is not every fresh revelation of the wishes of the loved one a fresh delight and privilege, and is any path found hard which their love compels them to travel?

Ah! Dear soul, if you have ever known this, even for a few hours, in any earthly relation; if you have ever loved any of your fellow human beings enough to find sacrifice and service on their behalf a joy; if a whole-souled abandonment of your will to the will of another has ever gleamed across you as a blessed and longed-for privilege or as a sweet and precious reality, then, by all the tender, longing love of your heavenly lover, would I entreat you to let it be so toward Christ!

He loves you with more than the love of friendship. As a bridegroom rejoices over his bride so does He rejoice over you, and nothing but the bride's surrender will satisfy Him. He has given you all, and He asks for all in return. The slightest reserve will grieve Him to the heart. He spared not Himself, and how can you spare yourself? For your sake He poured out in a lavish abandonment all that He had, and for His sake you must pour out all that you have, without stint or measure.

Oh, be generous in your self-surrender! Meet His measureless devotion for you with a measureless devotion to Him. Be glad and eager to throw yourself unreservedly into His loving arms and to hand over the reins of government to Him. Whatever there is of you, let Him have it all. Give up forever everything that is separate from Him. Consent to resign, from this time forward, all liberty of choice, and glory in the blessed nearness of union which makes this enthusiasm of devotedness not only possible, but necessary.

Have you never longed to lavish your love and attentions upon someone far off from you in position or circumstances with whom you were not intimate enough for any closer approach? Have you not felt a capacity for self-surrender and devotedness that has seemed to burn within you like a fire, and yet had no object upon which it dared to lavish itself? Have not your hands been full of "alabaster boxes of ointment, very precious," which you have never been near enough to any heart to pour out? If, then, you are hearing the loving voice of your Lord calling you out into a place of nearness to Himself that will require a separation from all else and that will make an enthusiasm of devotedness not only possible, but necessary, will you shrink or hesitate? Will you think it hard that He reveals to you more of His mind than He does to others, and that He will not allow you to be happy in anything that separates you from Himself? Do you *want* to go where He cannot go with you or to have pursuits which he cannot share?

No! No, a thousand times no! You will spring out to meet His lovely will with an eager joy. Even His slightest wish will become a binding law to you, that it would fairly break your heart to disobey. You will glory in the very narrowness of the path He marks out for you, and will pity with an infinite pity, the poor far-off ones who have missed this precious joy. The obligations of love will be to you its sweetest privileges; and the right you have acquired to lavish the uttermost wealth of abandonment of all that you have upon your Lord will seem to lift you into a region of unspeakable glory. The perfect happiness of perfect obedience will dawn upon your soul, and you will begin to know something of what Jesus meant when He said, "I *delight* to do thy will, O my God."

But do you think the joy in this will be all on your side? Has the Lord no joy in those who have thus surrendered themselves to Him and who love to obey Him? Ah, my friends, we are not able to understand this; but surely the scriptures reveal to us glimpses of the delight, the satisfaction, the joy our Lord has in us, which rejoice our souls with their marvelous suggestions of blessedness. That *we* should need Him is easy to comprehend; that *He* should need us seems incomprehensible. That our desire should be toward Him is a matter of course; but that His desire should be toward us passes the bounds of human belief. And yet He says it, and what can we do but believe Him? He has made our hearts capable of this supreme overmastering affection and has offered Himself as the object of it. It is infinitely precious to Him. So much does He value it, that He has made it the first and chiefest of all His commandments that we should love Him with all our might and with all our strength. Continually at every heart He is knocking, asking to be taken in as the supreme object of love. "Wilt thou have Me?" He says to the believer, "to be thy beloved? Wilt thou follow Me into suffering and loneliness and endure hardness for My sake and ask for no reward but My smile of approval and My word of praise? Wilt thou throw thyself, with a passion of abandonment, into My will? Wilt thou give up to Me the absolute control of thyself and of all that thou hast? Wilt thou be content with pleasing Me, and Me only? May I have My way with thee in all things? Wilt thou come into so close a union with Me as to make a separation from the world necessary? Wilt thou accept Me for thy heavenly bridegroom, and leave all others to cleave only to Me?"

In a thousand ways He makes this offer of union with Himself to every believer. But all do not say "Yes" to Him. Other loves and other interests seem to them too precious to be cast aside. They do not miss the joy of heaven because of this. But they miss an unspeakable present joy.

You, however, are not one of these. From the very first your soul has cried out eagerly and gladly to all His offers, "Yes, Lord, yes!". You are more than ready to pour out upon Him all your richest treasures of love and devotedness. You have brought to Him an enthusiasm of self-surrender that perhaps may disturb and distress the so-called prudent and moderate Christians around you. Your love makes necessary a separation from the world, of which a lower love cannot even conceive. Sacrifices and services are possible and sweet to you that could not come into the grasp of a more half-hearted devotedness. The life of love upon which you have entered gives you the right to a lavish outpouring of you *all* upon your beloved One. An intimacy and friendship, which more distant souls cannot enter upon, become now, not only your privilege, but your duty. Your Lord claims from you, because of your union with Him, far more than He claims of them. What to them is lawful, love has made unlawful of you. To you He can make known His secrets, and to you He looks for an instant response to every requirement of His love.

Oh, it is wonderful, the glorious, unspeakable privilege upon which you have entered! How little it will matter to you if men shall hate you and shall separate you from their company and shall reproach you and cast out your name as evil for His dear sake! You may well "rejoice in that day, and leap for joy," for behold, your reward is great in heaven; for if you are a partaker of His suffering, you shall also be of His glory.

In you He is seeing of the "travail of His soul" and is satisfied. Your love and devotedness are His precious reward for all He has done for you. It is unspeakably sweet to Him. Do not be afraid, then, to let yourself go in a heart-whole devotedness to your Lord that can brook *no* reserves. Others may not approve, but He will, and that is enough. Do not stint or measure your obedience or your service. Let your heart and your hand be as free to serve Him as His heart and hand were to serve you. Let Him have all there is of you, body, soul, mind, spirit, time, talents, voice, everything. Lay your whole life open before Him that He may control it. Say to Him each day, "Lord, enable me to regulate this day so as to please You! Give me spiritual insight to discover what is Your will in all the relations of my life. Guide me as to my pursuits, my friendships, my reading, my dress, my Christian work." Do not let there be a day nor an hour in which you are not consciously doing His will and following Him wholly.

A personal service to your Lord, such as this, will give a halo to the poorest life and gild the most monotonous existence with a heavenly glow. Have you ever grieved that the romance of youth is so soon lost in the hard realities of the world? Bring Christ thus into your life and into all its details and a romance, far grander than the brightest days of youth could ever know, will thrill your soul, and nothing will seem hard or stern again. The meanest life will be glorified by this. Often, as I have watched a poor woman at her washtub and have thought of all the disheartening accessories of such a life and have been tempted to wonder why such lives need to be, there has come over me, with a thrill of joy, the recollection of this possible glorification of it, and I have realized that even this homely life lived in Christ and with Christ, following Him whithersoever He might lead, would be filled with a spiritual romance that would make every hour of it grand; while to the most wealthy or most powerful of earthly lives, nothing more glorious could be possible.

Christ Himself, when He was on earth, declared the truth that there was no blessedness equal to the blessedness of obedience. "And it came to pass, as he spake these things, a certain woman of the company lifted up her voice, and said unto him, Blessed is the womb that bare thee, and the paps which thou hast sucked. But He said, Yea rather, blessed are they that hear the word of God, and keep it."

More blessed even than to have been the earthly mother of our Lord or to have carried Him in our arms and nourished Him in our bosoms (and who could ever measure the bliss of that?) is it to hear and obey His will!

May our surrendered hearts reach out with an eager delight to discover and embrace the lovely will of our loving God!

Chapter 18

Divine Union

A ll the dealings of God with the soul of the believer are in order to bring them into oneness with Himself, that the prayer of our Lord may be fulfilled; "That they all may be one; as thou, Father, art in me, and I in thee, that they also may be one in us. . . . I in them, and thou in me, that they may be made perfect in one; and that the world may know that thou hast sent me, and hast loved them, as thou hast loved me."

This divine union was the glorious purpose in the heart of God for His people before the foundation of the world. It was the mystery hid from ages and generations. It was accomplished in the death of Christ. It has been made known by the scriptures; and it is realized as an actual experience by many of God's dear children.

But not by all. It is true of all, and God has not hidden it or made it hard; but the eyes of many are too dim, and their hearts too unbelieving for them to grasp it. It is, therefore, for the purpose of bringing His people into the personal and actual realization of this that the Lord calls upon them so earnestly and so repeatedly to abandon themselves to Him that He may work in them all the good pleasure of His will.

All the previous steps in the Christian life lead up to

this. The Lord has made us for it; and until we have intelligently apprehended it and have voluntarily consented to embrace it, the "travail of His soul" for us is not satisfied, nor have our hearts found their destined and real rest.

The usual course of Christian experience is pictured in the history of the disciples. First they were awakened to see their condition and their need, and they came to Christ and gave their allegiance to Him. Then they followed Him, worked for Him, believed in Him; and yet how unlike Him they were! Seeking to be set up one above the other; running away from the cross; misunderstanding His mission and His words; forsaking their Lord in time of danger; they were still sent out to preach, recognized by Him as His disciples, and possessed power to work for Him. They knew Christ only "after the flesh," as outside of them, their Lord and Master, but not yet their life.

Then came Pentecost, and these same disciples came to know Him as inwardly revealed; as one with them in actual union, their very indwelling life. Henceforth He was to them Christ within, working in them to will and to do of His good pleasure, delivering them, by the law of the Spirit of His life, from the bondage to the law of sin and death under which they had been held. No longer was it, between themselves and Him, a war of wills and a clashing of interests. One will alone animated them, and that was His will. One interest alone was dear to them, and that was His. They were made *one* with Him.

And surely all can recognize this picture, though perhaps as yet the final stage of it has not been fully reached. You may have left much to follow Christ, dear reader; you may have believed on Him and worked for Him and loved Him, and yet may not be like Him. Allegiance you know, and confidence you know, but not yet union. There are two wills, two interests, two lives. You have not yet lost your own life that you may live only in His. Once it was "I and not Christ." Next it was "I and Christ." Perhaps now it is even "Christ and I." But has it come yet to be Christ only and not I at all?

If not, shall I tell you how it may? If you have followed me through all the previous chapters in this book, you will surely now be ready to take the definite step of faith, which will lead your soul out of self and into Christ, and you will be prepared to abide in Him forever and to know no life but His.

All you need, therefore, is to understand what the scriptures teach about this marvelous union, that you may be sure it is really intended for you.

If you read such passages as 1 Corinthians 3:16, "Know ye not that ye are the temple of God, and that the Spirit of God dwelleth in you?" and then look at the opening of the chapter and see to whom these wonderful words are spoken, even to "babes in Christ" who were "yet carnal" and walked according to men, you will see that this soul-union of which I speak, this unspeakably glorious mystery of an indwelling of God, is the possession of even the weakest and most failing believer in Christ; so that it is not a new thing you are to ask for but only to realize that which you already have. Of every believer in the Lord Jesus it is absolutely true that your "body is the temple of the Holy Ghost which is in you, which ye have of God."

But although this is true, it is also equally true that unless the believer knows it and lives in the power of it, it is to him as though it were not. Like the treasures under a man's field, which existed there before they were known or used by him, so does the life of Christ dwell in each believer as really before he knows it and lives in it as it does afterward; although its power is not manifested until, intelligently and voluntarily, the believer ceases from his own life and accepts

Christ's life in its place.

But it is very important not to make any mistakes here. This union with Christ is not a matter of emotions, but of character. It is not something we are to *feel,* but something we are to *be.* We may feel it very blessedly, and probably shall; but the vital thing is not the feeling, but the reality.

No one can be one with Christ who is not Christlike. This is a manifest truth; yet I fear it is often too much overlooked, and very strong emotions of love and joy are taken as signs and proofs of divine union in cases where the absolutely essential proofs of Christlike life and character are conspicuously wanting. This is entirely contrary to the scripture declaration that "he that *saith* he abideth in him ought himself also so to *walk,* even as he walked." There is no escape from this, for it is not only a divine declaration but is in the very nature of things as well.

We speak of being one with a friend, and we mean that we have a union of purposes and thoughts and desires. No matter how enthusiastic our friends may be in their expressions of love and unity, there can be no real oneness between us unless there are, at least in some degree, the same likes and dislikes, the same thoughts and purposes and ideals. Oneness with Christ means being made a "partaker of His nature," as well as of His life; for nature and life are, of course, one.

If we are really one with Christ, therefore, it will not be contrary to our nature to be Christlike and to walk as He walked, but it will be in accordance with our nature. Sweetness, gentleness, meekness, patience, long-suffering, charity, kindness will all be natural to the Christian who is a partaker of the nature of Christ. It could not be otherwise.

But people who live in their emotions do not always see this. They *feel* so at one with Christ that they look no farther than this feeling and often delude themselves with thinking they have come into the divine union, when all the while their nature and dispositions are still under the sway of self-love.

Now we all know that our emotions are most untrustworthy and are largely the result of our physical condition or our natural temperaments. It is a fatal mistake, therefore, to make them the test of our oneness with Christ. This mistake works both ways. If I have very joyous emotions, I may be deluded by thinking I have entered into the divine union when I have not; and if I have no emotions, I may grieve over my failure to enter when I really have entered.

Character is the only real test. God is holy and those who are one with Him will be holy, also. Our Lord Himself expressed His oneness with the Father in such words as these: "The Son can do nothing of himself, but what he seeth the Father do: for what things soever he doeth, these also doeth the Son likewise." "If I do not the works of my Father, believe me not. But if I do, though ye believe not me, believe the works: that ye may know, and believe, that the Father is in me, and I in him."

The test Christ gave, then, by which the reality of His oneness with the Father was to be known, was the fact that He did the works of the Father; and I know no other test for us now.

It is forever true in the nature of things that a tree is to be known by its fruits; and if we have entered into the divine union we shall bear the divine fruits of a Christlike life and conversation; for "he that saith, I know Him, and keepeth not His commandments, is a liar, and the truth is not in him. But whoso keepeth His word, in him verily is the love of God perfected: hereby know we that we are in Him."

"Hereby know we"; that is, by the "keeping of His word." Pay no regard to your feelings, therefore, in this matter of oneness with Christ but see to it that you have the really vital fruits of a oneness in character and walk and mind. Your emotions may be very delightful, or they may be very depressing. In neither case are they any real indications of your spiritual state. Very undeveloped Christians often have very powerful emotional experiences. I knew one who was kept awake often by the "waves of salvation," as she expressed it, which swept over her all night long, but who yet did not tell the truth in her interaction with others and was very far from honest in her business dealings. No one could possibly believe that she knew anything about a real divine union, in spite of all her fervent emotions in regard to it.

Your joy in the Lord is to be a far deeper thing than a mere emotion. It is to be the joy of knowledge, of perception, of actual existence. It is a far gladder thing to *be* a bird, with all the actual realities of flying, than only to *feel* as if you were a bird, with no actual power of flying at all. Reality is always the vital thing.

But now, having guarded against this danger of an emotional experience of divine union, let us consider how the reality is to be reached. And first I would say that it is not a new attitude to be taken by God but only a new attitude to be taken by us. If I am really a child of God, then of necessity my heart is already the temple of God, and Christ is already within me. What is needed, therefore, is only that I shall recognize His presence and yield fully to His control.

It seems to me just in this way. It is as though Christ were living in a house, shut up in a far-off closet, unknown and unnoticed by the dwellers in the house, longing to make Himself known to them, and to be one with them in all their daily lives and share in all their interests, but unwilling to force Himself upon their notice because nothing but a voluntary companionship could meet or satisfy the needs of His love. The days pass by over that favored household, and they remain in ignorance of their marvelous privilege. They come and go about all their daily affairs with no thought of their wonderful guest. Their plans are laid without reference to Him. His wisdom to guide and His strength to protect are all lost to them. Lonely days and weeks are spent in sadness, which might have been full of the sweetness of His presence.

But suddenly the announcement is made, "The Lord is in the house!" How will its owner receive the intelligence? Will he call out an eager thanksgiving and throw wide open every door for the entrance of his glorious guest? Or will he shrink and hesitate, afraid of His presence, and seek to reserve some private corner for a refuge from His all-seeing eye?

Dear friend, I make the glad announcement to you that the Lord is in your heart. Since the day of your conversion He has been dwelling there, but you have lived on in ignorance of it. Every moment during all that time might have been passed in the sunshine of His sweet presence, and every step have been taken under His advice. But because you knew it not and did not look for Him there, your life has been lonely and full of failure. But now that I make the announcement to you, how will you receive it? Are you glad to have Him? Will you throw wide open every door to welcome Him in? Will you joyfully and thankfully give up the government of your life into His hands? Will you consult Him about everything and let Him decide each step for you and mark out every path? Will you invite Him into your innermost chambers and make Him the sharer in your most hidden life? Will you say "Yes" to all His longing for union with you and with a glad and eager abandonment hand yourself and all that concerns you over into His hands? If you will, then shall your soul begin to know something of the joy of union with Christ.

But words fail me here! All that I can say is but a faint

picture of the blessed reality. For far more glorious than it would be to have Christ a dweller in the house or in the heart is it to be brought into such a real and actual union with Him as to be one with Him—one will, one purpose, one interest, one life. Human words cannot express such a glory as this. And yet it ought to be expressed, and our souls ought to be made so unutterably hungry to realize it that day or night we shall not be able to rest without it. Do you understand the words "one with Christ"? Do you catch the slightest glimpse of their marvelous meaning? Does not your whole soul begin to exult over such a wondrous destiny? It seems too wonderful to be true that such poor, weak, foolish beings as we are should be created for such an end as this; and yet it is a blessed reality. We are even *commanded* to enter into it. We are exhorted to lay down our own life that His life may be lived in us; we are asked to have no interests but His interests, to share His riches, to enter into His joys, to partake of His sorrows, to manifest His likeness, to have the same mind as He had, to think and feel and act and walk as He did.

Shall we consent to all this? The Lord will not force it on us, for He wants us as His companions and His friends, and a forced union would be incompatible with this. It must be voluntary on our part. The bride must say a willing "Yes" to the bridegroom, or the joy of their union is wanting. Can we not say a willing "Yes" to our Lord?

It is a very simple transaction and yet very real. The steps are but three: first, we must be convinced that the scriptures teach this glorious indwelling of God; then we must surrender our whole selves to Him to be possessed by Him; and finally, we must believe that He *has* taken possession and *is* dwelling in us. We must begin to reckon ourselves dead and to reckon Christ as our only life. We must maintain this attitude of soul unwaveringly. It will help us to say, "I am crucified with Christ: nevertheless I live; yet not I, but Christ liveth in me," over and over, day and night, until it becomes the habitual breathing of our souls. We must put off our self-life by faith continually and put on the life of Christ; and we must do this, not only by faith, but practically as well. We must continually put self to death in all the details of daily life and must let Christ instead live and work in us. I mean we must never do the selfish thing, but always the Christlike thing. We must let this become, by its constant repetition, the attitude of our whole being. And as surely as we do, we shall come at last to understand something of what it means to be made one with Christ as He and the Father are one. Christ left all to be joined to us; shall we not also leave all to be joined to Him in this divine union which transcends words but for which our Lord prayed when He said, "Neither pray I for these alone, but for them also which shall believe on me through their word; that they all may be one; as thou, Father, art in me, and I in thee; that they also may be one in us"?

Chapter 19

The Chariots of God

It has been well said that "earthly cares are a heavenly discipline"; but they are even something better than discipline—they are God's chariots sent to take the soul to its high places of triumph.

They do not look like chariots. They look instead like enemies, sufferings, trials, defeats, misunderstandings, disappointments, unkindnesses. They look like Juggernaut cars of misery and wretchedness, which are only waiting to roll over us and crush us into the earth. But could we see them as they really are, we should recognize them as chariots of triumph in which we may ride to those very heights of victory for which our souls have been longing and praying. The Juggernaut car is the visible thing; the chariot of God is the invisible. The King of Syria came up against the man of God with horses and chariots that could be seen by every eye, but God had chariots that could be seen by none save the eye of faith. The servant of the prophet could only see the outward and visible; and he cried, as so many have done since, "Alas, my master! how shall we do?" but the prophet himself sat calmly within his house without fear, because his eyes were opened to see the invisible; and all he asked for his servant was, "LORD, I pray thee, open his eyes, that he may see."

This is the prayer we need to pray for ourselves and for one another, "Lord, open our eyes that we may see"; for the world all around us, as well as around the prophet, is full of God's horses and chariots, waiting to carry us to places of glorious victory. And when our eyes are thus opened, we shall see in all the events of life, whether great or small, whether joyful or sad, a "chariot" for our souls.

Everything that comes to us becomes a chariot the moment we treat it as such; and on the other hand, even the smallest trials may be a Juggernaut car to crush us into misery or despair if we so consider them. It lies with each of us to choose which they shall be. It all depends not upon what these events are, but upon how we take them. If we lie down under them and let them roll over us and crush us, they become Juggernaut cars, but if we climb up into them, as into a car of victory, and make them carry us triumphantly onward and upward, they become the chariots of God.

Whenever we mount into God's chariots the same thing happens to us spiritually that happened to Elijah. We shall have a translation. Not into the heavens above us, as Elijah did, but into the heaven within us; and this, after all, is almost a grander translation than his. We shall be carried away from the low, earthly, groveling plane of life, where everything hurts and everything is unhappy, up into the "heavenly places in Christ Jesus," where we can ride in triumph over all below.

These "heavenly places" are interior, not exterior; and the road that leads to them is interior, also. But the chariot that carries the soul over this road is generally some outward loss or trial or disappointment; some chastening that does not indeed seem for the present to be joyous, but grievous; but that nevertheless afterward "yieldeth the peaceable fruit of righteousness unto them which are exercised thereby."

In the Canticles we are told of "chariots paved with love." We cannot always see the love-lining to our own particular chariot. It often looks very unlovely. It may be a cross-grained relative or friend; it may be the result of human malice or cruelty or neglect; but every chariot sent by God must necessarily be paved with love since God is love; and God's love is the sweetest, softest, tenderest thing to rest one's self upon that was ever found by any soul anywhere. It is His love, indeed, that sends the chariot.

Look upon your chastenings then, no matter how grievous they may be for the present, as God's chariots sent to carry your souls into the "high places" of spiritual achievement and uplifting, and you will find that they are, after all, "paved with love."

The Bible tells us that when God went forth for the salvation of His people, then he "did ride upon His horses and chariots of salvation"; and it is the same now. Everything becomes a "chariot of salvation" when God rides upon it. He maketh even the "clouds His chariots," we are told, and "rideth on the wings of the wind." Therefore the clouds and storms that darken our skies and seem to shut out the shining of the sun of righteousness are really only God's chariots into which we may mount with Him and "ride prosperously" over all the darkness. Dear reader, have you made the clouds in your life your chariots? Are you "riding prosperously" with God on top of them all?

I knew a lady who had a very slow servant. She was an excellent girl in every other respect and very valuable in the household; but her slowness was a constant source of irritation to her mistress, who was naturally quick, and who always chafed at slowness. This lady would consequently get out of temper with the girl twenty times a day, and twenty times a day would repent of her anger and resolve to conquer it, but in vain. Her life was made miserable by the conflict. One day it occurred to her that she had for a long while been praying for patience, and that perhaps this slow servant was the very chariot the Lord had sent to carry her soul over into patience. She immediately accepted it as such, and from that time used the slowness of her servant as a chariot for her soul; and the result was a victory of patience that no slowness of anybody was ever after able to disturb.

I knew another lady, at a crowded convention, who was put to sleep in a room with two others on account of the crowd. *She* wanted to sleep, but *they* wanted to talk; and the first night she was greatly disturbed and lay there fretting and fuming long after the others had hushed and she might have slept. But the next day she heard something about God's chariots, and at night she accepted these talking friends as her chariots to carry her over into sweetness and patience and was kept in undisturbed calm. When, however, it grew very late, and she knew they all ought to be sleeping, she ventured to say slyly, "Friends, I am lying here riding in a chariot!" The effect was instantaneous, and perfect quiet reigned! Her chariot had carried her over to victory, not only inwardly, but at last outwardly as well.

If we would ride in God's chariots, instead of our own, we should find this to be the case continually.

Our constant temptation is to trust in the "chariots of Egypt" or, in other words, in earthly resources. We can *see* them; they are tangible and real and look substantial; while God's chariots are invisible and intangible, and it is hard to believe they are there.

We try to reach high spiritual places with the "multitude of our chariots." We depend first on one thing and then on another to advance our spiritual condition and to gain our spiritual victories. We "go down to Egypt for help." And God is obliged often to destroy all our own earthly chariots before He can bring us to the point of mounting into His.

We lean too much upon a dear friend to help us onward in the spiritual life, and the Lord is obliged to separate us from that friend. We feel that all our spiritual prosperity depends on our continuance under the ministry of a favorite preacher, and he is mysteriously removed. We look upon our prayer meeting or our Bible class as the chief source of our spiritual strength, and we are shut up from attending them. And the "chariot of God" which alone can carry us to the place where we hoped to be taken by the instrumentalities upon which we have been depending is to be found in the very deprivations we have so mourned over. God must burn up with the fire of His love every chariot of our own that stands in the way of our mounting into His.

We have to be brought to the place where all other refuges fail us before we can say "He only." We say, "He *and* —something else," "He and my experience," or "He and my church relationships," or "He and my Christian work"; and all that comes after the "and" must be taken away from us or must be proved useless before we can come to the "He only." As long as visible chariots are at hand, the soul will not mount into the invisible ones.

Let us be thankful, then, for every trial that will help to destroy our earthly chariots and that will compel us to take refuge in the chariot of God which stands ready and waiting beside us in every event and circumstance of life. We are told that "God rideth upon the heavens"; and if we would ride with Him there, we need to be brought to the end of all riding upon the earth.

When we mount into God's chariot our goings are "established," for no obstacles can hinder His triumphal course. All losses, therefore, are gains that bring us to this. Paul understood this, and he glorified in the losses which brought him such unspeakable rewards. "But what things were gain to me, those I counted loss for Christ. Yea doubt-less, and I count all things but loss for the excellency of the knowledge of Christ Jesus my Lord: for whom I have suf-fered the loss of all things, and do count them but dung, that I may win Christ, and be found in him."

Even the "thorn in the flesh," the messenger of Satan sent to buffet him, became a "chariot of God" to his willing soul and carried him to the heights of triumph, which he could have reached in no other way. To "take pleasure" in one's tri-als, what is this but to turn them into the grandest chariots?

Joseph had a revelation of his future triumphs and reign-ing, but the chariots that carried him there looked to the eye of sense like dreadful Juggernaut cars of failure and defeat. Slavery and imprisonment are strange chariots to take one to a kingdom, and yet by no other way could Joseph have reached his exaltation. And our exaltation to the spiritual throne that awaits us is often reached by similar chariots.

The great point, then, is to have our eyes opened to see in everything that comes to us a "chariot of God," and to learn how to mount into these chariots. We must recognize each thing that comes to us as being really God's chariot for us and must accept it as from Him. He does not command or originate the thing, perhaps; but the moment we put it into His hands, it becomes His, and He at once turns it into a chariot for us. He makes all things, even bad things, work together for good to all those who trust Him. All He needs is to have it entirely committed to Him.

When your trial comes, then, put it right into the will of God and climb into that will as a little child climbs into its mother's arms. The baby carried in the chariot of its mother's arms rides triumphantly through the hardest places and does not even know they are hard. And how much more we, who are carried in the chariot of the "arms of God"!

Get into your chariot, then. Take each thing that is wrong in your lives as God's chariot for you. No matter who the builder of the wrong may be, whether men or devils, by the time it reaches your side it is God's chariot for you and is meant to carry you to a heavenly place of triumph. Shut out all the second causes and find the Lord in it. Say, "Lord, open my eyes that I may see, not the visible enemy, but thy unseen chariots of deliverance."

No doubt the enemy will try to turn your chariot into a Juggernaut car by taunting you with the suggestions that God is not in your trouble, and that there is no help for you in Him. But you must utterly disregard all such suggestions and must overcome them with the assertion of a confident faith. "God *is* my refuge and strength, a very present help in trouble," must be your continual declaration, no matter what the seemings may be.

Moreover, you must not be half-hearted about it. You must climb wholly into your chariot, not with one foot dragging on the ground. There must be no "ifs" or "buts" or "supposings" or "questionings." You must accept God's will fully and must hide yourself in the arms of His love that are always underneath to receive you in every circumstance and at every moment. Say, "Thy will be done; Thy will be done," over and over. Shut out every other thought but the one thought of submission to His will and of trust in His love. There can be no trials in which God's will has not a place somewhere; and the soul has only to mount into His will as in a chariot, and it will find itself "riding upon the heavens" with God in a way it had never dreamed could be.

The soul that thus rides with God "on the sky" has views and sights of things that the soul which grovels on the earth can never have. The poor crushed and bleeding victim under the car of Juggernaut can see only the dust and stones and the grinding wheels, but the triumphant rider in the chariot sees far fairer sights.

Do any of you ask where your chariots are to be found? The psalmist says, "The chariots of God are twenty thousand, even thousands of angels." There is never in any life a lack of chariots. One dear Christian said to me at the close of a meeting where I had been speaking about these chariots: "I am a poor woman and have all my life long grieved that I could not drive in a carriage like some of my rich neighbors. But I have been looking over my life while you have been talking, and I find that it is so full of chariots on every side that I am sure I shall never need to walk again."

I have not a shadow of doubt, dear readers, that if all our eyes could be opened today we should see our homes and our places of business and the streets we traverse filled with the "chariots of God." There is no need for any one of us to walk for lack of chariots. That cross inmate of your household, who has hitherto made life a burden to you and who has been the Juggernaut car to crush your soul into the dust, may henceforth be a glorious chariot to carry you to the heights of heavenly patience and long-suffering. That misunderstanding, that mortification, that unkindness, that disappointment, that loss, that defeat—all these are chariots waiting to carry you to the very heights of victory you have so longed to reach.

Mount into them then, with thankful hearts, and lose sight of all second causes in the shining of His love, who will "carry you in His arms" safely and triumphantly over it all.

Chapter 20

The Life on Wings

This life hid with Christ in God has many aspects and can be considered under a great many different figures. There is one aspect which has been a great help and inspiration to me, and I think may be also to some other longing and hungry souls. It is what I call the life on wings.

Our Lord has not only told us to consider the "flowers of the field," but also the "birds of the air"; and I have found that these little winged creatures have some wonderful lessons for us. In one of the Psalms, the psalmist, after enumerating the darkness and bitterness of his life in this earthly sphere of trial, cries out, "Oh that I had wings like a dove! for then would I fly away, and be at rest. Lo, then would I wander far off, and remain in the wilderness. . . . I would hasten my escape from the windy storm and tempest" (Psalm 55:6–8).

This cry for "wings" is as old as humanity. Our souls were made to "mount up with wings," and they can never be satisfied with anything short of flying. Like the captive-born eagle that feels within it the instinct to flight and chafes and frets at its imprisonment, hardly knowing what it longs for, so do our souls chafe and fret and cry out for freedom. We can never rest on earth, and we long to "fly away" from all that so holds and hampers and imprisons us here.

This restlessness and discontent develop themselves generally in seeking an outward escape from our circumstances or from our miseries. We do not at first recognize the fact that our only way of escape is to "mount up with wings," and we try to "flee on horses," as the Israelites did, when oppressed by their trials (see Isaiah 30:16).

Our "horses" are the outward things upon which we depend for relief, some change of circumstances or some help from man; and we mount on these and run east or west, or north or south, anywhere to get away from our trouble, thinking in our ignorance that a change of our environment is all that is necessary to give deliverance to our souls. But all such efforts to escape are unavailing as we have each one proved hundreds of times; for the soul is not so made that it can "flee upon horses" but must make its flight always upon wings.

Moreover, these "horses" generally carry us, as they did the Israelites, out of one trouble, only to land us in another. It is, as the prophet says, "As if a man did flee from a lion, and a bear met him; or went into the house, and leaned his hand on the wall, and a serpent bit him."

How often have we also run from some "lion" in our pathway only to be met by a "bear"; or have hidden ourselves in a place of supposed safety, only to be bitten by a "serpent"! No; it is useless for the soul to hope to escape by running away from its troubles to any earthly refuge, for there is not one that can give it deliverance.

Is there, then, no way of escape for us when in trouble or distress? Must we just plod wearily through it all and look for no relief? I rejoice to answer that there is a glorious way of escape for every one of us if we will but mount up on wings and fly away from it all to God. It is not a way east or west, or north or south, but it is a way upwards. "They that wait upon the LORD shall renew their strength; they shall mount up with wings as eagles; they shall run, and not be weary; and they shall walk, and not faint."

All creatures that have wings can escape from every snare that is set for them if only they will fly high enough, and the soul that uses its wings can always find a sure "way to escape" from all that can hurt or trouble it.

What, then, are these wings? Their secret is contained in the words, "They that wait upon the Lord." The soul that waits upon the Lord is the soul that is entirely surrendered to Him and that trusts Him perfectly. Therefore, we must name our wings the wings of Surrender and of Trust. I mean by this, that, if we will only surrender ourselves utterly to the Lord and will trust Him perfectly we shall find our souls "mounting up with wings as eagles" to the "heavenly places" in Christ Jesus, where earthly annoyance or sorrows have no power to disturb us.

The wings of the soul carry it up into a spiritual plane of life, into the "life hid with Christ in God," which is a life utterly independent of circumstances, one that no cage can imprison and no shackles bind.

The "things above" are the things the soul on wings cares about, not the "things on the earth"; and it views life and all its experiences from the high altitude of "heavenly places in Christ Jesus." Things look very different according to the standpoint from which we view them. The caterpillar, as it creeps along the ground, must have a widely different "view" of the world around it from that which the same caterpillar will have when its wings are developed, and it soars in the air above the very places where once it crawled. And, similarly, the crawling soul must necessarily see things in a very different aspect from the soul that has "mounted up with wings." The mountain top ablaze with sunshine when all the valley below is shrouded in fogs and the bird whose wings can carry him high enough may mount at will out of the gloom below into the joy of the sunlight above.

I was at one time spending a winter in London, and during three long months we did not once see any genuine sunshine because of the dense clouds of smoke that hung over the city like a pall. But many a time I have seen that above the smoke the sun was shining, and once or twice through a rift I have had a glimpse of a bird, with sunshine on its wings, sailing above the fog in the clear blue of the sunlit sky. Not all the brushes in London could sweep away the fog; but could we only mount high enough, we should reach a region above it all.

And this is what the soul on wings does. It overcomes the world through faith. To overcome means to "come over," not to be crushed under; and the soul on wings flies over the world and the things of it. These lose their power to hold or bind the spirit that can "come over" them on the wings of Surrender and Trust. That spirit is made in very truth "more than conqueror."

Birds overcome the lower law of gravitation by the higher law of flight; and the soul on wings overcomes the lower law of sin and misery and bondage by the higher law of spiritual flying. The "law of the spirit of life in Christ Jesus" must necessarily be a higher and more dominant law than the law of sin and death; therefore, the soul that has mounted into this upper region of the life in Christ cannot fail to conquer and triumph.

But it may be asked how it is, then, that all Christians do not always triumph. I answer that it is because a great many Christians do not "mount up with wings" into this higher plane of life at all. They live on the same low level with their circumstances; and instead of flying over them, they try to fight them on their own earthly plane. On this plane the soul is powerless; it has no weapons with which to conquer there; and instead of overcoming, or coming over, the trials and sorrows of the earthly life, it is overcome by them and crushed under them.

We all know, as I have said, that things look differently to us according to our "point of view." Trials assume a very different aspect when looked down upon from above than when viewed from their own level. What seems like an impassable wall on its own level becomes an insignificant line to the eyes that see it from the top of a mountain; and the snares and sorrows that assume such immense proportion while we look at them on the earthly plane become insignificant little notes in the sunshine when the soul has mounted on wings to the heavenly places above them.

A friend once illustrated to me the difference between three of her friends in the following way. She said, if they should all three come to a spiritual mountain which had to be crossed, the first one would tunnel through it with hard and wearisome labor; the second would meander around it in an indefinite fashion, hardly knowing where she was going, and yet, because her aim was right, getting around it at last; but the third, she said, would just flap her wings and fly right over. I think we must all know something of these different ways of locomotion; and I trust, if any of us in the past have tried to tunnel our way through the mountains that have stood across our pathway or have been meandering around them, that we may from henceforth resolve to spread our wings and "mount up" into the clear atmosphere of God's presence, where it will be easy to overcome, or come over, the highest mountain of them all.

I say "spread our wings and mount up," because not the largest wings ever known can lift a bird one inch upward unless they are used. We must *use* our wings or they avail us nothing.

It is not worthwhile to cry out, "Oh that I had wings, and then I would flee"; for we *have* the wings already, and what is needed is not more wings, but only that we should use those we have. The power to surrender and trust exists in every human soul and only needs to be brought into exercise. With these two wings we *can* "flee" to God at any moment; but, in order really to reach Him, we must actively use them. We must not merely want to use them, but we must *do* it definitely and actively. A passive surrender or a passive trust will not do. I mean this very practically. We shall not "mount up" very high if we only surrender and trust in theory or in our especially religious moments. We must do it definitely and practically, about each detail of daily life as it comes to us. We must meet our disappointments, our thwartings, our persecutions, our malicious enemies, our provoking friends, our trials and temptations of every sort, with an active and experimental attitude of surrender and trust. We must spread our wings and "mount up" to the "heavenly places in Christ" above them all, where they will lose their power to harm or distress us. For from these high places we shall see things through the eye of Christ, and all earth will be glorified in the heavenly vision.

> *The dove hath neither claw nor sting,*
> *Nor weapon for the fight,*
> *She owes her safety to the wing,*
> *Her victory to flight.*
> *The Bridegroom opens His arms of love,*
> *And in them folds the panting dove.*

How changed our lives would be if we could only fly through the days on these wings of surrender and trust! Instead of stirring up strife and bitterness by trying, metaphorically, to knock down and walk over our offending brothers and sisters, we should escape all strife by simply spreading our wings and mounting up to the heavenly region where our eyes would see all things covered with a mantle of Christian love and pity.

Our souls were made to live in this upper atmosphere, and we stifle and choke on any lower level. Our eyes were made to look off from these heavenly heights, and our vision is distorted by any lower gazing. It is a great blessing, therefore, that our loving Father in heaven has mercifully arranged all the discipline of our lives with a view to teaching us to fly.

In Deuteronomy we have a picture of how this teaching is done: "As an eagle stirreth up her nest, fluttereth over her young, spreadeth abroad her wings, taketh them, beareth them on her wings: so the LORD alone did lead him, and there was no strange god with him."

The mother eagle teaches her little ones to fly by making their nest so uncomfortable that they are forced to leave it and commit themselves to the unknown world of air outside. And just so does our God to us. He stirs up our comfortable nests and pushes us over the edge of them, and we are forced to use our wings to save ourselves from fatal falling. Read your trials in this light and see if you cannot begin to get a glimpse of their meaning. Your wings are being developed.

I knew a lady whose life was one long strain of trials from a cruel, wicked, drunken husband. There was no possibility of human help, and in her despair she was driven to use her wings and fly to God. And during the long years of trial her wings grew so strong from constant flying that at last, as she told me, when the trials were at their hardest, it seemed to her as if her soul was carried over them on a beautiful rainbow and found itself in a peaceful resting place on the other side.

With this end in view we can surely accept with thankfulness every trial that compels us to use our wings, for only so they can grow strong and large and fit for the highest flying. Unused wings gradually wither and shrink and lose their flying power; and if we had nothing in our lives that made flying necessary, we might perhaps at last lose all capacity to fly.

But you may ask, Are there no hindrances to flying, even where the wings are strong, and the soul is trying hard to use them? I answer, Yes. A bird may be imprisoned in a cage, or it may be tethered to the ground with a cord, or it may be loaded with a weight that drags it down, or it may be entrapped in the "snare of the fowler"; and hindrances which answer to all these in the spiritual realm may make it impossible for the soul to fly until it has been set free from them by the mighty power of God.

One "snare of the fowler" that entraps many souls is the snare of doubt. The doubts look so plausible and often so humble that Christians walk into their "snare" without dreaming for a moment that it is a snare at all until they find themselves caught and unable to fly; for there is no more possibility of flying for the soul that doubts than there is for the bird caught in the fowler's snare.

The reason of this is evident. One of our wings, namely, the wing of trust, is entirely disabled by the slightest doubt; and just as it requires two wings to lift a bird in the air, so does it require two wings to lift the soul. A great many people do everything but trust. They spread the wing of surrender and use it vigorously and wonder why it is that they do not mount up, never dreaming that it is because all the while the wing of trust is hanging idle by their sides. It is because Christians use one wing only that their efforts to fly are often so irregular and fruitless.

Look at a bird with a broken wing trying to fly, and you

will get some idea of the kind of motion all one-sided flying must make. We must use both our wings or not try to fly at all.

It may be that for some the "snare of the fowler" is some subtle form of sin, some hidden want of consecration. Where this is the case, the wing of trust may seem to be all right, but the wing of surrender hangs idly down; and it is just as hopeless to try to fly with the wing of trust alone as with the wing of surrender alone. Both wings must be used, or no flying is possible.

Or perhaps the soul may feel as if it were in a prison from which it cannot escape and consequently is debarred from mounting up on wings. No earthly bars can ever imprison the soul. No walls, however high, or bolts, however strong, can imprison an eagle, so long as there is an open way upward; and earth's power can never hold the soul in prison while the upward way is kept open and free. Our enemies may build walls around us as high as they please, but they cannot build any barrier between us and God; and if we "mount up with wings," we can fly higher than any of their walls can ever reach.

If we find ourselves imprisoned, then, we may be sure of this, that it is not our earthly environment that constitutes our prison-house, for the soul's wings scorn all paltry bars and walls of earth's making. The only thing that can really imprison the soul is something that hinders its upward flight. The prophet tells us that it is our iniquities that have separated between us and our God, and our sins that have hid His face from us. Therefore, if our soul is imprisoned, it must be because some indulged sin has built a barrier between us and the Lord, and we cannot fly until this sin is given up and put out of the way.

But often, where there is no conscious sin the soul is still unconsciously tethered to something of earth and so struggles in vain to fly. A party of my friends once got into a boat in Norway to row around one of the fiords there. They took their seats and began to row vigorously, but the boat made no headway. They put out more strength and rowed harder than before, but all in vain; not an inch did the boat move. Then one of the party suddenly recollected that the boat had not been unmoored, and he exclaimed, "No wonder we could not get away, when we were trying to pull the whole continent of Europe after us!" And just so our souls are often not unmoored from earthly things. We must cut ourselves loose. As well might an eagle try to fly with a hundred-ton weight tied fast to its feet, as the soul try to "mount upon with wings" while a weight of earthly cares and anxieties is holding it down to earth.

When our Lord was trying to teach His disciples concerning this danger, He told them a parable of a great supper to which many who were invited failed to come because they were hindered by their earthly cares. One had bought a piece of ground, another a yoke of oxen, and a third had married a wife; and they felt that all these things needed their care.

Wives or oxen or land, or even very much small things, may be the cords that tether the soul from flying or the weights that hold it down. Let us then cut every cord and remove every barrier that our souls may find no hindrance to their mounting up with wings as eagles to heavenly places in Christ Jesus.

We are commanded to have our hearts filled with songs of rejoicing and to make inward melody to the Lord. But unless we mount up with wings this is impossible, for the only creature that can sing is the creature that flies. When the prophet declared that though all the world should be desolate, yet he would rejoice in God and joy in the God of his salvation, his soul was surely on wings. Paul knew what it was to use his wings when he found himself to be "sorrowful, yet always rejoicing." On the earthly plane all was dark to both Paul and the prophet, but on the heavenly plane all was brightest sunshine.

Do you know anything of this life on wings, dear reader? Do you "mount up" continually to God, out of and above earth's cares and trials, to that higher plane of life where all is peace and triumph; or do you plod wearily along on foot through the midst of your trials and let them overwhelm you at every turn?

Let us, however, guard against a mistake here. Do you think that by flying I mean necessarily any very joyous emotions or feelings of exhilaration. There is a great deal of emotional flying that is not real flying at all. It is such flying as a feather accomplishes which is driven upward by a strong puff of wind, but flutters down again as soon as the wind ceases to blow. The flying I mean is a matter of *principle,* not a matter of *emotion.* It may be accompanied by very joyous emotions, but it does not depend on them. It depends only upon the facts of an entire surrender and an absolute trust. Every one who will honestly use these two wings and will faithfully persist in using them, will find that they *have* mounted up with wings as an eagle, no matter how empty of all emotion they may have felt themselves to be before.

For the promise is sure: "They that wait upon the LORD *shall* mount up with wings as eagles." Not "may perhaps mount up," but *"shall."* It is the inevitable result. May we each one prove it for ourselves!

> The lark soars singing from its nest,
>   And tells aloud
> His trust in God, and so is blest
>   Let come what cloud.
> He has no store, he sows no seed,

Yet sings aloud, and doth not heed.
Through cloudy day or scanty feed,
    He sings to shame
Men who forget in fear of need
    A Father's name.

The heart that trusts, forever sings,
And feels as light as it has wings;
A well of peace within it springs.
    Come good or ill,
Whate'er today or morrow bring,
    It is His will.

BELOVED CHRISTIAN CLASSICS
Only $4.97 each!

At the Back of the North Wind
by George MacDonald
ISBN 1-59310-681-5
Who is this mysterious and beautiful North Wind?
Find out in the classic allegory by George MacDonald,
one of the primary influences of C. S. Lewis.

In the Twinkling of an Eye
by Sydney Watson
ISBN 1-59310-683-1
Long before there was *Left Behind*, there was *In the Twinkling of an Eye*—read this classic novel for another perspective on Christ's return!

In His Steps
by Charles M. Sheldon
ISBN 1-59310-682-3
Read the classic novel that asks the question
"What would Jesus do?"—the book that's changed
countless lives over the past hundred years.

The Pilgrim's Progress
by John Bunyan
ISBN 1-59310-684-X
Find out why the simple story of Christian,
the Pilgrim, making his way to the Celestial City,
has entranced readers for more than
three hundred years.

Available from Barbour Publishing
wherever books are sold.

Inspiring Christian Classics

Grow in your daily walk with Christ with these classic Christian writings that have stood the test of time. The classic-looking, hardback format is designed to last—and offered at the tremendous value of just $7.97 each!

The Christian's Secret of a Happy Life
ISBN 1-59310-707-2
In need of spiritual victory? Let Hannah Whitall Smith share the "secrets" of freedom—from the bondage of sin, to the life of Christ.

Daily Thoughts for Disciples
ISBN 1-59310-706-4
Those who love Oswald Chambers for *My Utmost for His Highest* now have another devotional option—*Daily Thoughts for Disciples*, compiled from Chambers's many books.

Foxe's Christian Martyrs
ISBN 1-59310-710-2
Power up your own faith by reading the dramatic stories of early Christian martyrs—from the time of the apostles through the sixteenth century.

Morning by Morning
ISBN 1-59310-711-0
See why nineteenth century preacher Charles Spurgeon is still popular, by starting your day with his *Morning by Morning* devotionals.

With Christ in the School of Prayer
ISBN 1-59310-709-0
Want to know how to pray? Let Andrew Murray, the foremost authority on the deeper Christian life, take you to Jesus' "school of prayer."

The Wonderful Names of Our Wonderful Lord
ISBN 1-59310-708-0
Take a one-year course in knowing Jesus with this 365-day devotional based on the biblical names of Christ. You'll be enlightened and encouraged!

Available from Barbour Publishing
wherever books are sold.

ISBN 1-59310-707-2

EAN

9 781593 107079